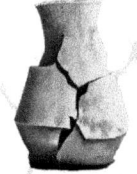

CRACKED VESSELS

True Stories of Real Life Restoration

J.P. and Diana Spitz
With Mark Ellis

CRACKED VESSELS
Copyright 2024 by J.P. and Diana Spitz
ISBN: 978-1-964359-01-4
LCCN: 2024915825

All rights reserved. No part of this book may be reproduced, stored in a retrieval system, or transmitted in any form or by any means—electronic, mechanical, digital, photocopy, or any other—without prior permission from the publisher and author, except as provided by the United States of America copyright law.

Unless otherwise noted, all scriptures are from the NEW KING JAMES VERSION®. Copyright© 1982 by Thomas Nelson, Inc. Used by permission. All rights reserved.

Scripture quotations marked (NIV) are taken from THE HOLY BIBLE, NEW INTERNATIONAL VERSION®. Copyright© 1973, 1978, 1984, 2011 by Biblica, Inc.™. Used by permission of Zondervan.

Scripture quotations marked (NASB) are taken from the NEW AMERICAN STANDARD BIBLE®, Copyright© 1960, 1962, 1963, 1968, 1971, 1972, 1973, 1975, 1977, 1995 by The Lockman Foundation. Used by permission.

Address all personal correspondence to:
D. Spitz, c.o. Kathy's House
P.O. Box 1466
San Juan Capistrano, CA 92693
www.kathyshouse.org

Individuals and church groups may order books from the authors directly, or from the publisher. Retailers and wholesalers should order from our distributors. Refer to the Deeper Revelation Books website for distribution information, as well as an online catalog of all our books.

Published by:
Deeper Revelation Books
Revealing "the deep things of God" (1 Cor. 2:10)
P.O. Box 4260
Cleveland, TN 37320 423-478-2843
Website: www.deeperrevelationbooks.org
Email: info@deeperrevelationbooks.org

Deeper Revelation Books assist Christian authors in publishing and distributing their books. Final responsibility for design, content, permissions, editorial accuracy, and doctrinal views, either expressed or implied, belongs to the author. What you hold in your hands (or what you are viewing in an e-book format) is an expression of this author's passion to publish the truth with a spirit of excellence. It was a blessing and an honor to help in the process.

Endorsements

J.P. and Diana have devoted their lives to serving God and helping the poor and needy. They've dreamed big and worked hard and kept at it decade after decade. What a joy to read stories of how God redeems, saves, and uses ordinary people like J.P. and Diana who are willing to take risks and say yes to God. I hope this book inspires many people to also say yes to God and experience a life of adventure in God's work.

Pastor Roger Gales
Heritage Christian Fellowship Church

...

J.P. and Diana know what it is to never quit on the needy. This book is full of amazing stories of never giving up. Enjoy.

Pastor Jason Welsh
Amazing Church, Lake Elsinore

Dedication

We dedicate this book to our Lord and our family.

Our Children:
Lisa, Joey, Jill & Paul.

Our Grandchildren:
Jack, Mark, Robert, Ciara, Beth, Yancey, Rachel, Samantha & Seth.

Our Great-Grandchildren:
Rachel, Noah, Abby, Zachery, William, Colton, Drew & Olivia.

Authors' Note

We have chosen to tell our collection of testimonies using a first-person voice. We each share our personal testimonies. J.P. then narrates the chapters detailing his trips to Pakistan, while Diana narrates all the remaining chapters. May God bless you as you read our stories.

J.P. and Diana Spitz

Table of Contents

Chapter 1
Final Negotiation 15

Chapter 2
Diana's Story 17

Chapter 3
J.P.'s Story 29

Chapter 4
Jenna's Miracle 41

Chapter 5
Untimely Passing 43

Chapter 6
How We Met 47

Chapter 7
Uncommon Honeymoon 51

Chapter 8
Learning to Forgive 55

Chapter 9
Launching a Ministry 59

Chapter 10
Taking in a Troubled Young Man 65

Chapter 11
Beans, Rice, and Jesus Christ 69

Chapter 12
Jenna's Struggle 73

Chapter 13
An Eleventh-Hour Prayer 79

Chapter 14
Charlie's Funeral 83

Chapter 15
Ministry Life 87

Chapter 16
Children Belong to God 91

Chapter 17
No God Wanted 93

Chapter 18
A Wedding Made Complete 95

Chapter 19
Launching Kathy's House Ministry 97

Chapter 20
Lori's Story 101

Chapter 21
Terry Martin's Passing 109

Chapter 22
Jonathan's Story 113

Chapter 23
Feeding Sudan 125

Chapter 24
Jason's Story 129

Chapter 25
A Tragic Accident 137

Chapter 26
Eric's Story 139

Chapter 27
The Call to Pakistan 149

Chapter 28
Second Pakistan Visit 155

Chapter 29
Third Pakistan Visit 159

Chapter 30
The Miraculous Fourth Visit 163

Chapter 31
Transitions 179

Chapter 32
Beyond the Finish Line 191

Final Thoughts 189

Afterword 195

Endnotes 197

About the Authors 199

Chapter 1

Final Negotiation

It was Ramadan, the month-long period of fasting by Muslims that commemorates the revelation of the Quran to Muhammad.

I, Joseph Paul ("J.P."), and another man from our church, Mark, two intrepid travelers, had traveled over 8,000 miles to Pakistan on a special mission—to free as many as 4,500 Christian slaves from a brick factory. We would be using $96,000, wondrously raised in a church of 400 at one service a few weeks before the trip.

Soon after our arrival, we went to the brick factory to see the owner, who happened to be a member of the Taliban. "I don't want to talk here," the man told us. "I want you to come to my farmhouse at 6:00 tonight."

At 6 p.m., the Taliban owner called and said he couldn't make it but would call when he was ready. At 9 p.m., we started to get nervous, knowing so many lives were at stake.

"I'm afraid to go over there," I admitted to Pastor Tariq, the local church leader who served as our liaison. "This guy is evil." Pastor Tariq said he wanted to get the deal done that night.

Finally, the Taliban leader called at 9:30 and told us to come to his farmhouse. It was pitch black as we approached the man's home. A guard came out to the gate carrying a 57-magnum pistol.

I was in the lead car along with Mark, Pastor Tariq, and a security guard carrying an AK-47. A second car followed with three pastors on Pastor Tariq's board and another security guard. A third car was filled with four security guards equipped with AK-47s.

As we pulled up, an amber porch light revealed the house was heavily guarded by more Taliban with AK-47s. We were ushered into a room with one door, two windows without glass, and a desk. The night air was heavy.

Mark and I sat on one side of the desk, and Pastor Tariq stood at the end. The three pastors were standing against the wall. The Taliban leader and his secretary sat on the other side of the desk. Their guards and our guards were standing around. The guy guarding the door was very evil-looking. The secretary looked very evil.

Immediately the Taliban leader declared he wanted $1,000 per family—a dramatic increase over the agreed terms of $250. The secretary asked if Pastor Tariq brought cash with him.

"No, it's in the bank," Pastor Tariq replied.

The secretary turned red and pounded the table. "We want cash, cash, cash," he roared.

"You ought to give them to us for free because of all the money they've made for you over the years," Mark blurted out.

One of the Taliban leader's guards started shouting, then got up and stuck the barrel of his AK-47 against one pastor's throat.

This is going to be a bloodbath. I waited for the room to erupt in gunfire.

...

How did a seventy-three-year-old retired barber, former pastor, and businessman find himself in Pakistan negotiating late at night with the Taliban for the release of Christian slaves toiling in Pakistani brick factories?

We'll answer that question, but first, discover how God molded and shaped my wife, Diana, and me using us as His instruments of grace to reach the last, the least, and the hopelessly lost who crossed our paths.

Chapter 2
Diana's Story

I was born Diana Arias and grew up Catholic, attending a parochial school in Southern California. My mother, Orfelia, was a former Miss Latin America with a Hollywood movie contract. She was so beautiful, but she married and divorced five times. It was hard to call each man Daddy because I didn't think of them as my daddy.

In my lineage, I am directly related to the former president of Mexico, Álvaro Obregón. My aunt is the only living relative from that generation, and I asked her about it. She said yes, we are related to him, but it's not what you think.

I got hints of the story from my grandmother. Occasionally while I was growing up, she would show me checks from Mexico made out in her name—her name was Obregón.

Álvaro Obregón was originally a farmer in Sonora, became a general in the Mexican Revolution, then became the forty-sixth President of Mexico, serving from 1920 to 1924.

During a battle with Pancho Villa, an explosion blew off Obregón's right arm, nearly killing him. Reeling in shock and horror at his mutilated condition, he reached for his sidearm to kill himself, but an aide who had cleaned the weapon failed to replace the bullets. Instead, Obregón began a frantic search with others for his missing arm.

John F. W. Dulles, in the opening lines of his book *Yesterday in Mexico: A Chronicle of the Revolution, 1919 to 1936*, quotes Obregón's dark humor about the unusual hunt: "I was helping them myself, because it's not so easy to abandon such a necessary thing as an arm." The searchers were not having any luck, though. Then a comrade reached into his pocket and raised a gold coin. Obregón concluded the story: "And then everyone saw a miracle: the arm came forth from who knows where, and came skipping up to where the gold *azteca* [coin] was elevated; it reached up and grasped it in its fingers—lovingly—That was the only way to get my lost arm to appear."[1]

After being out of office for several years, Obregón launched a contentious campaign in 1927 to regain the presidency. Obregón became associated with the anti-Catholic strain of the Revolution. After he successfully won the election and returned to Mexico City in 1928, he was assassinated as he sat in La Bombilla Café by a fervent supporter of the Roman Catholic Church.

The true mastermind of Obregon's killing was a nun named María Concepción Acevedo de la Plata, the "Madre Conchita," according to Jaymie Heilman's journal article "The Demon Inside: Madre Conchita, Gender, and the Assassination of Obregon."[2]

In a somewhat macabre twist, Obregón's arm was embalmed and put on display at a monument to his life at the Parque de la Bombilla where he was assassinated.

His life contains a remarkable parallel to the biblical King Saul, who rose from humble beginnings as a farmer and became a military commander and ultimately the ruler of his people.

My aunt was able to unlock the history of our family ties. She told me the story of how he was a teacher originally and a farmer, and he had a ranch where he grew peas. He met my great-grandmother when he was a schoolteacher. She was also a teacher, and they fell in love, but he was married to someone else. He had two children by her, my grandmother and her brother. When she was twelve years old, he had them sent to the

United States. He said he would take care of them, and the checks did come each month for my grandmother from Mexico. She would show me her support checks.

We have a photo on the wall in our home of Pancho Villa with my great-grandfather, taken "before things went bad."

Like my great-grandfather, I had a tenuous relationship with the Roman Catholic Church. Being Catholic meant nothing to me. I didn't know who Jesus was in parochial school. I wore the school uniform, and nuns were doing the teaching, but I didn't feel they were educating me other than making me fearful of them. I knew there was another person up there in heaven, but I didn't know who Jesus was. I would walk into church and see all these horrible depictions of Jesus with blood dripping down from his hands and feet, but I had no clue what it meant.

After my sister, Norma, was born, my father forced my mother to have an abortion when she got pregnant again because he didn't want any more children. Because of his pressure, our younger brother was never born.

When I was five, my mother dropped Norma and me at our grandmother's house and then went missing for a week. When my mom finally returned, I happened to have a bloody nose and was confined to a bedroom. There were two policemen in the living room talking to my mom. I wanted to be with my mom, but I had a bloody nose, and my grandmother wouldn't let me near her.

My father refused to work and instead became a perpetual student. He loved being in school. He wanted to be a doctor, then decided he wanted to be a psychologist. Mom worked to support us, and he refused to do anything but go to school. He made my mother the breadwinner. He said he was not Hispanic. He had my birth certificate altered so it didn't say Mexican.

Later I learned when my mother separated from my father, he became enraged and kidnapped her. He had a gun and was going to kill her.

To escape, my mother deceived him by pretending she had a change of heart and still had feelings for him. She told him they would live "happily ever after."

She convinced my father she just needed to pick up us girls at grandma's house. He dropped her off at my grandmother's house and waited in the car. But once she got inside, they locked up the house and called the police. That was a traumatic memory.

After my mom returned home, my father was arrested and went to prison, sentenced to twenty years. After I was separated from my father for many years, God placed in my heart a desire to know my father. I started praying when I was sixty to meet my father. I wanted to see him face to face.

A year after I began diligently praying about him, my sister got an unexpected phone call from one of our cousins. Our father had been asking about finding us. We met and talked to him about kidnapping my mother, and he denied all of it. He said he had never been in prison. He said maybe two men had the same last name. But we had seen his records and knew he was in prison.

For a year, my sister took care of him in her home. She was divorced and had the time to do that. J.P. and I both worked full-time. The doctor said he had congestive heart failure and would only live another six months at the most. He died while COVID-19 was roaring. We tried to visit him once a month, but our fear of passing COVID-19 to him was a constant worry. I tried to warm up to him, and I did at first, but he continued to tell us lies. He was not a good man. My sister would take him grocery shopping, and if someone was in his way, he would shove them aside. He was very rude.

We talked once in a while, and then he died. My

mother had already passed from complications of Alzheimer's when we met him. I didn't want her to be alive when we met him because of the awful things he had done to her.

When I was twelve, my mother worked as a dental assistant but made arrangements to take off two months in the summer so she could move to Las Vegas. There she became a blackjack dealer to earn extra money. She would have me stay with one of my aunts. I would be so angry she was leaving me again during the summer. She got more money, but we still had the same lifestyle.

While there, she met and married a man named Mario, the piano player at the Sands Hotel. They got married in Vegas. We didn't know Mario, her second husband, was bipolar. I didn't even know what bipolar or ADHD was, or even an alcoholic, but we had plenty of them in the family.

Their marriage was short-lived. His mental instability began to unnerve everyone in the home. I would open a closet door in the hallway, and a noose would be hanging there. He wanted to kill himself.

One morning Mario tried to gas himself to death using the car's exhaust in the garage. I said goodbye to him before I went to school, and he was in the garage gassing himself. I didn't know he was doing that. I said, "I'm going to school now," but he didn't answer me. I left and later came home to an empty house. He was gone and so *was* my mother.

After I returned from school, a neighbor came over. She told me she was supposed to watch me until my mother came home.

"What happened?" I asked.

"Your stepfather tried to kill himself using the car exhaust in the garage, but he survived," she said to my shock and dismay.

Shortly after that, I found more nooses in the closets

and confronted my mother. "Why is he doing this? What is wrong with him?" I pleaded.

Mom sighed and with resignation said, "He has a mental disorder."

One morning my mother informed us, "Okay, girls, we are leaving today. We're not going to tell him we're leaving. I am telling him we're going to visit Grandma in Pico Rivera. I want you to pack your favorite clothes, not a lot, and take one of your favorite toys."

I grabbed a stuffed skunk I got in Las Vegas. We lived at my grandmother's for a week, but then Mario tracked us down and knocked at the front door.

He begged my mother to take him back and said things would change and be different. At that point, I was very afraid of him. After three days of begging, he convinced my mother to go back to him.

Then my mother did a horrible thing that left me an emotional scar. My mother told Mario if I wanted to come back, they would come back. She put it on ME. I couldn't believe she was doing that. I kept telling her not to go back, to stay here. I was even more afraid of him because the decision was put on me. I gave in and said, "Fine, we can go back." I WAS SO SCARED! We got in the car and waved goodbye to Grandma.

The four of us started driving, with Mario at the wheel. I was sitting in the back seat. He pulled out a gun and pointed it at me.

"When we get to Vegas, I'm going to use this gun on you," he coldly informed me.

During the interminable seven-hour drive, he had the gun on me. I know my mother was thinking, "Why did I do this?" But there was nothing we could do, all the way to Las Vegas.

As soon as we arrived at the house in Las Vegas and stepped out of the car, Mom yelled, "Girls, run!"

We got out of the back of the car and started running down the street. My mom was running with us. I looked back, and he was running after us. A man was mowing his yard, and my mom said, "Please, can we hide in your house?" He said no and walked away. We kept running and running. We looked back, and he wasn't running after us anymore.

"Quick, let's get in the backyard of this home," Mom said.

A woman, who turned out to be a teacher on her lunch break, stepped out of the house. "What's going on?" she asked.

"We're running from my husband, and he has a gun!" Mom shouted.

"Come in the house quickly and call the police, and we'll get you some help," she said.

After the police arrived, they escorted my family and I back to the house. They didn't see him or his gun anywhere. They waited while we packed everything we had. They put us on a Greyhound bus back to Grandma's where we started a new life living with her. My admiration for law enforcement grew tremendously after that experience and influenced my decision years later when I married a police officer.

A short time later, my mother met a man named Morrie in Las Vegas and decided to marry him. These men would be attracted to her because she was beautiful. They would convince her to marry them, and she hardly knew them at all.

They moved to Garden Grove where Morrie bought a home. I was doing reasonably well in high school, but my mother and her new husband were not. My sister was chubby at the time, and he started calling her names. I thought it was rude for an adult to do that.

My mother often worked late because the dental office remained open until 8 p.m. He was very jealous and would show up at night and look through the windows to see what she was doing. He was obsessed with the idea that she was unfaithful.

My aunt Betty married a man from New York we called Uncle Whitey because he had white hair. One weekend my mother sent us two girls to stay with our aunt, uncle, and cousins, but she left out one important detail: Aunt Betty was in the hospital.

We were all helping to make dinner. Uncle Whitey was an Italian from New York and always seemed to be screaming. I had never been around that kind of person before. I thought it was so strange. He told me to go to the garage and get the spaghetti sauce out of the freezer. He wanted to thaw it so he could make us a spaghetti dinner. I went in there, and he followed quietly behind me. When we were alone in the garage, he grabbed me from behind, pulled me toward him, and started rubbing my breasts. I pulled away ... it scared me to death!

I went into the house and frantically called my mother. I said, "Mom, you need to come and get me. I don't want to be here anymore."

My mother refused. I didn't tell her what he did. I just said I didn't want to be there alone with Uncle Whitey with Aunt Betty in the hospital. She wouldn't do it. I don't remember what reason she gave. From that point on, he didn't go near me, and I avoided him.

I first married at nineteen, but the marriage only lasted three years.

I met my second husband, a police officer named Paul, while I worked in the finance department in the city of Huntington Beach, California. A coworker brokered our introduction. I had been single for a while. I was lonely, so I agreed to meet him.

He called me that night and asked me out, and we married six months later.

Paul and I bought a ranch in Northern California

because Paul wanted to be a rancher. Things went well for a while, but then I got sick. Doctors suspected cancer. I traveled back to Orange County to have a hysterectomy. My two children and I stayed with my sister while I recuperated. My stitches broke, and I hemorrhaged. I kept hemorrhaging and had to be taken to the hospital twice.

As I convalesced, I noticed something strange. My husband wasn't calling to check on me very much. He was up in Yreka, running the farm. We had sixty head of beef cattle. He was feeding them and taking care of the ranch. I noticed his phone calls were rare.

Even though I wasn't supposed to travel, I felt the urgent need to return home and persuaded my stepfather, Robert, to drive me up to Yreka—a fourteen-hour drive.

After I returned home, I confronted my husband. I said, "What's going on, Paul? You're not calling me."

Then he delivered the hammer blow. "I want a divorce," he told me.

When I asked why, he said, "I don't want to be married anymore. I just want a divorce."

"Let's talk and wait a couple of weeks," I implored.

After a few days, I noticed he was coming home for lunch, looking for something in the mailbox. Later I realized we hadn't received our phone bill.

I called the phone company, and they sent me a copy. As I scanned the bill, I saw numerous calls to a phone number in the next town over. I picked up the phone and called the number. A woman answered, and I hung up.

I showed him the phone bill, and he knew he was done. I was devastated, crying. He finally confessed it was a woman he met at a Christmas party. He got drunk, and they got together. He was quite a playboy. This was a pattern I didn't know about when we first married. He said he didn't want to be with her; he wanted to be with me.

We lived amid the tension of a deeply violated trust for a little while. We got a phone call, and it was her. I heard him whispering to her.

I went into the room where he was talking and said, "I want you to tell her it's over. I want to be in the room when you tell her that."

I heard Paul tell his girlfriend the relationship was over and he was going to stay with me.

Then I grabbed the phone and said, "I'm his wife. You need to know we have two children. I don't want him to leave me. I love him. It was a fling on his part, and we'd like you to leave us alone."

"He told me he was in the middle of a divorce," the woman said weakly. "I will not bother you anymore."

She didn't bother us, but the violation of trust lingered, souring the marriage. He started thinking he wanted out. We separated. He quit the police department because police departments were very strict in those days.

Eventually he had another affair, and I thought I couldn't live this way. It broke my heart all over again. I called Mom and Dad and packed up the clothing we had. I got in the car with our clothes and the kids and drove back to Huntington Beach. They had an apartment there and took us in. That was the end of that.

I was thirty-five and going through a divorce, completely devastated. I thought the marriage was going to be for life. I was single for fourteen years because I was afraid of men in general. I didn't want to get hurt anymore.

After the divorce, my best girlfriend Margie started calling me and would quote Bible verses which she felt would help my feelings of despair. I told her I didn't want to hear that and the verses wouldn't help me.

Still, I would cry on her shoulder and tell her all my woes. She would call me again and give me another Bible verse.

One day I called her and, to her surprise, asked if she could give me another Bible verse. I told her they had been helping me. The scriptures ministered so much to me and got me through that period of my life.

When I visited my mother and stepfather in Diamond Bar, I saw they were attending a home church down the street led by Dr. Jack Welch, who became a good friend and a mentor to me.

My mother invited me to Easter service at the home church, and I wore a big Easter hat. My kids loved Sunday school in the garage. While I was sitting there, I started weeping uncontrollably. I was embarrassed because I was crying so much. The Easter message touched me, and I remember thinking I could now get healing. I had been miserable.

The Holy Spirit came upon me, and I said yes to Jesus. I left that place a born-again Christian. I could not stop crying. Jack said I had been touched by the Holy Spirit.

I grew and grew as a Christian. I studied the whole Bible in and out. Pastor Jack was a big Bible reader. I am not a very social person, so the closeness of that fellowship was incredible. Jack and his wife Pat became my mentors. I saw how they raised their children. I saw the love they shared with the thirty people in that small, sweet fellowship.

Chapter 3

J.P.'s Story

I was born in the small, unincorporated town of Morgan, Missouri—a town so small it lost its post office in the mid-seventies. I was the youngest of six children.

At my birth in 1943, World War II was still raging in Europe and the Pacific. My parents decided to move to Southern California where they landed jobs supporting the war effort, my father in the shipyards and my mother working on aircraft.

One of my early traumatic memories involved my oldest brother, Wayne, dying tragically from a burst appendix at the formative age of seventeen, shortly after he was engaged to be married. It was the custom in those days to lay the body out for viewing, and people went in to mourn. Wayne was laid out on the kitchen table. My twelve-year-old brother was terrified. People would come over and cry and bring food.

I admit to inheriting many of my father's traits. He was competitive, not even letting his grandkids win at a game of checkers.

I remember a wonderful childhood growing up in National City, a town within the greater San Diego area which boasts a three-mile-long port area forming part of the U.S. naval base. I don't ever remember coming home when my father and mother weren't there.

Both my parents found Jesus as teenagers at a revival meeting in Missouri and followed a strict, traditional set of values, not allowing alcohol in the house. Everybody in the family came to our house on the weekend, but my mother and father didn't have many friends outside the family.

I excelled in basketball and in my senior year of high school received promising news: I not only was accepted to La Verne College but also would receive an athletic scholarship.

However, the family was jolted by an unwelcome development. I got my girlfriend, Carol, pregnant in our senior year, 1960. That was kind of traumatic. I had been my dad's favorite. Before this happened, he told me that because of my scholarship, he would pay all my college expenses, including my car insurance and gas.

My father confronted me about the pregnancy. He said, "Well, what are you going to do, son?"

"Well," I stammered, "I still want to go to college. I want to go up there and bring Carol, and we'll get married."

"Oh no, son," my father replied. "Listen, when you stuck that pecker in the hole, you became a family man. Now you have to go to work and make your mark."

I had been receiving a five-dollar weekly allowance from my parents, plus an additional five dollars each week to eat lunch in the cafeteria. To save money, I ate at home, so I cleared ten dollars—not nearly enough to support a wife.

When I turned eighteen, I landed a job at Rohr Aircraft operating their drop hammer. Pioneered by Fred Rohr in the 1930s, the 30,000-pound metal press revolutionized the way aluminum aircraft parts were made. They started me at $1.50 an hour, but after only two months I was laid off. If they waited three months, I would have joined the union, and I would have gotten classified.

My brother Bill, a barber, encouraged me to consider a different direction. He said, "If you go to barber school, I'll give you a job. You'll never have to worry about a job again because people get their hair cut all the time." So, I went to barber school and got my first job in East L.A.

I followed the honorable course and married Carol.

Tragically, Carol suffered a miscarriage several days after our nuptials.

We moved to Baldwin Park, founded by Elias Baldwin, one of California's more colorful businessmen and land speculators. Shortly after we arrived, I engaged in some exuberant celebrations at a New Year's Eve party and came to work the next day hungover.

Assessing my sluggish deportment, the barber cutting hair next to me said, "Here, take this," handing me "bennies" or "uppers," a methamphetamine precursor. They made me feel good.

I worked seven days a week for over a year and saved enough money to buy my first barbershop in Pomona. I was a young punk who thought I knew everything. By that time, I was doing drugs every day. I was drinking Jim Beam whiskey to come down. I would do three or four bennies a day. In the end, I was doing fifty to sixty a day because my body was building up a tolerance.

I was high all the time and loved it because I could work all the time. What you do is tweak. "Tweaking" is a slang term that describes the unusual behavior of methamphetamine addicts. An addict is described as a tweaker; you fixate on stuff. I did that for years. I bought huge jars full of bennies, 2,000 in a jar. It didn't take long for me to realize I had a compulsive addictive personality.

When methamphetamine users go on a binge fueled by the stimulant, they may not sleep for days, and then become irritable, unpredictable, or even psychotic when they finally come down. I used whiskey to cushion the fall and avoid the "goofy" behavior.

Despite my addiction, I did well in business and began to acquire more barbershops. I thought if I could get two barbershops, I could afford a house, and if I can get three, I wouldn't have to work.

At home, Carol struggled with health issues. I didn't know she had diabetes until the day after we got married.

She had one child but couldn't have another because she was a severe diabetic. The doctor said her life expectancy was forty-two. In those days the medications would destroy your organs.

When I discovered the seriousness of Carol's diabetes, I didn't know how to deal with it. It shook me up. I sold my two barbershops, bought a brand-new 1965 Oldsmobile, and we took a year to travel. I bought a trailer, and we started in Mexico and went up to Lake Louise in Canada.

I was never going to ever own another barbershop again. I was just going to cut hair and fill in.

After a year we returned, and I found a job cutting hair in San Diego. However, I couldn't resist the strong urge to own my own business. I met a man who owned several barbershops, including a highly lucrative one in Leisure World (now Laguna Woods) that employed ten barbers every day.

I approached the owner and said, "I would like to buy your barbershop in Leisure World."

"It's not for sale," the man replied.

"Everything is for sale," I retorted.

"If it was for sale, it would be $40,000," the man said, confident that would end the discussion.

"Okay, I'll give you $40,000," I said, knowing I only had $8500. Then I asked if the man would carry paper—allow seller financing.

We struck a phenomenal deal for $40,000, in which I would give him $10,000 down and pay $500 a month on the balance. But I needed to borrow an additional $1500. I called my brother Bill, and he said no.

"You're going to have to talk to Dad," he told me.

That was the last thing I wanted to do. When I was

eighteen, I wanted to buy a Chevy Nova in the worst way. I called my father and asked if he would co-sign on a note.

"I've never had a house payment (or any debt), and if you're going to do that, I don't want any part of it," my dad replied gruffly.

I cursed my father and hung up on him. I didn't get the Chevy Nova, and I didn't talk to him for over a year.

Now years later, I didn't want to call him to ask for money. Finally, I gathered my courage, placed the call, and made an impassioned plea.

"Yeah, I hear you need to buy a barbershop and don't have the money," my father said. "I can tell you right now I'm not going to lend you the money, I'm going to give it to you, son. You have proven to me you're going to be okay."

It was a healing moment in our relationship that meant the world to me.

Over time, I began to acquire more barbershops. I stopped cutting hair and devoted my time to managing the shops. Despite my financial acumen, my pill addiction was festering. I would go out and drink and come home late at night. I drank when I was coming down off the meth so I wasn't goofy. Carol didn't know I was using drugs. She was raised Lutheran and was very naive. In those days people didn't do drugs. This was before the hippies.

One night I came home high. I had been drinking to come down. I got in bed, and Carol started talking about her girlfriend Sue.

"I went over to Sue's house today, and I can't figure her out," she said. "Her husband has a lousy job, she doesn't have a car, and they don't own their home ..." By comparison, we had attained much more in a material sense.

"Sue, why are you so happy?" Carol asked her friend.

"Because Jesus lives in me," she said.

That night, Carol turned to me in bed and asked, "How could Jesus live in someone?"

"I don't know," I said, mystified.

Until that moment, I had never given much thought to religion or God. I didn't think that way. Different people had witnessed to me, but it didn't hit me at all. I thought they were weird. Reflecting on my life, however, I knew I was coming to the end of my rope. We had applied to the County of Orange to adopt a little girl. I was drunk the day they came to inspect the house, so they put a stop to it. They didn't say no; they said I needed to go to counseling.

Before I went to sleep that night, I offered up a prayer to God: "Jesus, if You're for real, would You come into my heart and take over my life?" By the time I woke up the next morning, a spirit of repentance had fallen on me. The Holy Spirit convicted me of my sinful condition. I felt dirty inside and knew I needed to get off the drugs.

Over the next two months, a baby girl named Jill was placed in our home on a probationary basis. I fell in love with her. She was the cutest little thing. One day the adoption home inspectors visited, and I had been drinking.

Carol got angry and spilled the beans. In a moment of unexpected candor, she told the person inspecting our home that I had violated the terms of our agreement. The inspector gave me a cold look and said, "You're in hot water, buddy. You need to get help."

I made a commitment to do something, and I was terrified. Nobody had heard of AA. I called a hotline, and they told me I had to be hospitalized to get off the drugs. I thought I couldn't do that because everybody would find out.

On the following Sunday morning, I took a dramatic step. I flushed all my drugs down the toilet. That was scary. Before this, I would shake if I didn't have the drugs.

Carol had gone to church by herself that morning, to Gloria Dei Lutheran Church in Dana Point. I felt compelled to join her and made my way to their outdoor chapel where I dropped to my knees and began to pray earnestly: "God, You've gotta help me ..."

Choked with emotion, I couldn't get any more words out and began to cry. All of a sudden, Jesus became real to me. I couldn't explain what was happening.

The Holy Spirit of the living God fell upon me, and I was born again, as the Gospel of John describes:

> *Jesus replied, "Very truly I tell you, no one can see the kingdom of God unless they are born again."*
>
> *"How can someone be born when they are old?" Nicodemus asked. "Surely, they cannot enter a second time into their mother's womb to be born!"*
>
> *Jesus answered, "Very truly I tell you, no one can enter the kingdom of God unless they are born of water and the Spirit. Flesh gives birth to flesh, but the Spirit gives birth to spirit. You should not be surprised at my saying, 'You must be born again.' The wind blows wherever it pleases. You hear its sound, but you cannot tell where it comes from or where it is going. So it is with everyone born of the Spirit."* (John 3:3–8 NIV)

I felt unburdened, a new sense of freedom, and an inner peace I had never felt before. I had a monkey off my back, and I knew I was going to be okay. Remarkably, when I was born again and threw away the drugs, I was completely healed of my addiction and never had to detox. The desire for alcohol, cigarettes, and drugs was all gone, a miraculous outcome not always shared by those who struggle with addiction.

I came home excited to tell Carol what happened. But when I confessed the serious nature of my addiction—hidden from her for a long time—she was furious. She got angry and took the kids, Joey and Jill, to her mother's house in Chula Vista. She said, "I'm never coming back."

Our separation was brief; it only lasted one day.

I started reading the New Testament, and when I got to the third chapter of John, I knew it described what had happened to me. That's when my Christian life started.

The regeneration of my heart brought a change at work. I had a barbershop in Garden Grove, and we had six barbers. None of them were Christians, and we drank every day. When we closed, the person who finished first had to buy for everyone else. I would always get a pint of Jim Beam whiskey. They asked if I wanted the same thing, Jim Beam, and I said, "I don't feel very good. I'm going to pass." At that point, I didn't have what it took to say what happened to me.

One of the men who got his hair cut at my shop, Mr. Seaman, owned a stationery store in the same shopping center. He also happened to be a strong Christian. He would witness to all of us, and I never paid any attention to it. No one did. We made fun of him.

I remembered Mr. Seaman sold Bibles in his stationery store. I went in to buy a Bible and put one up on the counter. He came to ring me up and asked, "Are you a Christian?"

"Yes," I replied meekly.

"Praise God, hallelujah!" he exclaimed. His eyes filled with excitement and joy.

Still timid and somewhat embarrassed about what happened to me, I left the store quickly.

A short time later a hippie came limping into the barbershop for a haircut, wearing a cast on his leg. He asked me to cut off all his hair, something you didn't do in those days.

"Why are you getting it cut off?" I asked. "And what happened to your leg?"

"I was high on LSD and thought I could fly, so I jumped out of a two-story building and broke my leg. My parents have been fighting me about this hair. I've been on a lot of LSD trips, but something happened to me, and I want to prove to them I'm changed."

"What changed?"

"When I went into the emergency room for my leg, the nurse told me about Jesus." Then the young man turned and looked at me with a goofy-looking grin and invited me to Calvary Chapel Costa Mesa, led by Pastor Chuck Smith.

I accepted the invitation and arrived early because I had been warned it would be packed. It was all hippies. Chuck was sitting on the pulpit, and he had a big belly, his T-shirt was too small, and he had the same goofy grin. I was down in the front row because we got there early.

When the singing began, everyone stood up, locked arms, and started swaying together. At first it was too much for me, and I thought I had to get out of there. But that first worship song, led by the Rotinos, talking about how Jesus was the Savior of my soul, melted my heart.

I got into it and started going around to any church that I could, just because it was a church.

I had been playing handball at San Clemente High School with a youth pastor named Homer Waisner. He was on fire for the Lord. One day Homer invited me to pass out hot chocolate to students at San Clemente High. We set up tables, and Homer would get somebody and walk them to their class, telling them about Jesus. I couldn't do it, so I sat down on the curb while he was witnessing boldly.

Homer walked up to me and asked, "What's the matter?"

I said, "I see what you're doing, and I want to do it, but I can't. I'm embarrassed …"

"You need to be plugged into the Holy Ghost," Homer said. "You've got no power in your life."

A few weeks later I attended a service with a guest speaker from Philadelphia, Father Mike Gatos, who was born blind and had been miraculously healed by the Lord. He didn't have pupils in his eyes, and they were discolored like marbles. Also, he didn't have distinct eyelids. He started talking about how Jesus restored his eyesight. Everybody said, "Oh my God—He's healed!"

Because of Carol's advancing diabetes, she was slowly losing her eyesight. I approached Father Gatos and asked him to pray for her.

Father Gatos looked at me and asked something unexpected: "Have you been baptized in the Holy Spirit?"

I thought that was quite a thing to ask when I was asking for prayer for healing.

"Would you like to be baptized in the Holy Spirit?" he asked.

"Yeah, okay," I said.

"Let's just worship the Lord," Father Gatos said. He began singing, "Hallelujah."

I started singing, and my tongue got twisted.

Father Gatos started laughing. "Let it go!" he bellowed. All of a sudden it was like a fire hydrant was blown off me.

"J.P.!" Carol exclaimed in embarrassment, not fully understanding or accepting what was happening.

I went home and couldn't stop singing to the Lord and speaking in tongues. The next morning, I led my first barbershop customer to Jesus Christ. From then on, I probably should have been locked up. Filled with a newfound boldness from the Holy Spirit, I became a witnessing machine, urging others to find new life in Christ.

Chapter 4
Jenna's Miracle

Doctors told Carol and I she couldn't have a baby because of her severe diabetic condition. They said it might kill her and the baby.

Carol already had a stroke and a mild heart attack. She went blind the year after we were saved. She was only twenty-eight. Not a person to wallow in self-pity, she did very well. When she got pregnant, the doctor mentioned to us the baby had no more than a five percent chance to live. After seven and a half months of pregnancy, the doctors took the baby early.

We named our miracle baby Jenna. When Jenna was four months, we went up to Forest Home, a Christian retreat and conference center in the local mountains. While we were there, the camp suffered a power outage, and we resorted to using flashlights after dark. We shined a light in Jenna's eyes because the whole cabin was dark. She didn't move or follow the light. She just stared blankly at us. That was our first inkling something was wrong.

When we returned home, we immediately arranged an appointment with a pediatric ophthalmologist, who delivered heartbreaking news. He said her macula (the oval-shaped area at the center of the retina) was *not* deformed, but her brain was not communicating with the eye via the optic nerve. He said it was a condition doctors can't do anything about. The optical nerve is the smallest in the body. If it's damaged or does not develop properly, it always results in irreversible blindness.

We got despondent. During a Christmas visit with my parents in National City, they placed Jenna in a small swing in the living room. They had this huge Christmas tree with lights, and she didn't look at it. It was depressing. We started going to doctors to see if something could be done.

A few weeks later, I was driving and became emotional about my wife and daughter. I pulled over and started crying out to the Lord. I said, "God, this isn't fair. I have a blind wife, and now I have a blind baby. God, if you want me to have a blind baby and a blind wife, I will accept that. But God, in Your mercy, please send healing."

A short time later, my parents arrived for a visit. It was early in the morning. Jenna started crying, and I went up to get her. She was in a crib, and we had a mobile hanging over her. She started grabbing for it. She turned and looked at me. Pretty soon her head was bobbing everywhere. She could see! God answered our prayers and healed baby Jenna's eyesight.

We went to church on the next Sunday, I held her up and said, "She can see!!!" It was just an amazing miracle!

Chapter 5

Untimely Passing

Sadly, in Carol's late thirties, she began to experience severe diabetes complications that resulted in kidney damage. Damage to her eyes, known as diabetic retinopathy, had already caused blindness. Damage to her kidneys, known as diabetic nephropathy, now required dialysis.

By forty-two, Carol was in a terrible condition. She was in the hospital on the dialysis machine and not doing well. The staff called me on a Sunday morning and told me to come in right away. They called a code blue, which meant everybody rushed into the room to keep her alive. They had paddles and would shock her. She came back ten or eleven times. Her organs were failing.

I entered her hospital room, drew close to her, and pressed my face next to hers.

"Where am I?" she asked softly.

"You're in room 323," I said.

"No," she said, "I'm on a train with Robbie Young, and it's very bright."

Robbie Young was a young man who lived next door to Carol when she was growing up. He had been the quarterback on our high school football team. I was a halfback on the same team.

She told me she was on a train, and it was very bright. Then she passed into the arms of her Savior.

Afterward, I wondered whether Carol was hallucinating and thought her vision may have been a result of the medications given her at the end.

We had a glorious funeral. Later I went to visit her

mother, Lillian, who lived in National City. As I traveled south on the San Diego Freeway, it suddenly occurred to me that I should take flowers to Carol's mother. So, I pulled off the freeway in Del Mar and went into a Ralphs supermarket to buy flowers.

Standing in line, I noticed a woman who looked familiar but whom I hadn't seen in years. I wasn't sure who she was. I asked, "Excuse me, are you Mrs. Young ... Robbie Young's mother?"

"Yes, I am," she replied to my astonishment.

"I married Carol Flanders," I told her.

"How is Carol?" she asked.

"I'm sad to say she died a week ago."

"Oh, I'm so sorry to hear about that."

"How are Robbie and Judy doing?"

"Robbie has been the biggest heartache in my life. He moved up to Livermore, California. He started drinking and hanging out in bars. He left Judy and ran away with a lady bartender. He didn't take care of his kids and didn't support her. He died of cancer not that long ago."

"I'm sorry to hear that," I said.

After I got home, I decided I would attempt to reach Robbie's widow.

I called information, got the number for Robbie Young, and dialed. A woman answered the phone. I said, "My name is J.P., and I was a friend of Robbie. I heard he died recently ..."

"Yes," she said. "Robbie and I messed up two families. I left my kids and husband, and he left his wife. We started doing drugs. We got messed up, and he got cancer. But by the grace of God, we became Christians."

"Let me tell you about my wife Carol and her last words," I said and proceeded to share the story of her final moments.

"You don't know how badly I needed to hear that," she said.

I marveled at God's grace and His impeccable timing in the way He brings people together at such moments. What were the chances of me meeting Mrs. Young in Del Mar? That's miles away—a whole different world than National City. The Bible says one day is like a thousand years, and a thousand years is like one day (2 Peter 3:8).

Chapter 6
How We Met

I (Diana) spent many years after my painful divorce with little or no interest in dating or marrying again. My childhood traumas, witnessing my mother's failed marriages, and suffering the severe betrayal of trust due to my spouse's adultery left me jaded about men.

I began working for one of the pastors at Mariners Church in Newport Beach. He was very active, spoke at many churches, traveled around the United States, and wrote several books.

I saw red flags when he became unusually close to his administrative assistant and seemed to be paying more attention to her than to his wife. He also started counseling a very wealthy woman. They wound up leaving their spouses and married. That experience increased my guardedness about men.

Fourteen years after my divorce, I attended a friend's wedding at Mariners. I was a guest of the groom, a church friend. We sang in the choir together. I was talking to my friend Margie as the wedding started, and she looked over my shoulder and said, "That's Paul, and you have to meet him. He's a great guy, he's available, and he owns a gas station." (He actually owned a barbershop.)

At the reception, Paul, aka J.P., spotted Margie and ambled over to say hello.

"You've got to meet Paul," Margie said to me as she introduced the two of us. J.P. sat down next to me, and something remarkable happened.

The still small voice of the Lord spoke to J.P.'s heart. *This is the woman you're going to marry.*

At that moment, however, I didn't hear anything from God and wasn't particularly interested in J.P. During the reception when the time came to cut the wedding cake, Paul walked over to me again, and we talked for a bit.

I told Margie not to give him my phone number. I had no interest in dating anyone at the time.

But J.P. was persistent, driven by the assurance he got from the Lord and the attractive qualities he said he saw in me. After we began dating, I began to warm up to J.P.'s heart. What I liked about J.P. is that he loved people. He wanted to get serious, but I told him we should just be friends and not go that far.

In addition to his business ventures, J.P. had become the pastor of care and counseling at Ocean Hills Church. At that time, the church was meeting in a gymnasium at Dana Hills High School. After Carol's passing, he had two children at home, Jill, seventeen, and Jenna, eight. Joey, twenty-one, was away at college. Many of his friends were trying to fix him up with someone.

We got engaged but kept it a secret from the congregation. J.P. was running the service one Sunday after our engagement and said something to the effect that we have a lot of new people here this morning and some of us don't know each other. So he went down the center aisle with the mic introducing new people, and then he came to me.

"Gosh, I haven't seen you here at church," J.P. said. "Can you tell me something about yourself?"

The audience was laughing because they knew J.P. was single and had an interest in me —they could tell.

"Gosh, maybe we could get together sometime," J.P. continued. Are you doing anything on Saturday, June 26?

"Yes, as a matter of fact, I'm marrying you!" I said as a big smile broke out on my face.

The whole auditorium roared.

We married seven months after our first meeting. I was shaking when I went to my wedding rehearsal because I was terrified of marriage. But I saw his heart and how much he loved people.

I went into the marriage with two children, Lisa, eighteen, and Paul, fifteen. Lisa had just graduated and was on her own, but Paul was living at home.

CRACKED VESSELS

Chapter 7

Uncommon Honeymoon

We did not go to one of the usual honeymoon spots some might consider their dream destination like Hawaii, the Caribbean, or Europe. A week after our wedding, we jetted to South Korea with a group from the church on a mission trip. J.P. is very frugal, so he counted our mission trip to Yonggi Cho's church in South Korea as our honeymoon.

In 1958, Pastor David Yonggi Cho founded the Yoido Full Gospel Church with his mother-in-law, meeting in her home with just a few people. After extensive canvassing of the neighborhood, the church grew to fifty and began to meet in a tent in the backyard. After outgrowing several tents, they built their first church in a district near the heart of Seoul, the capital.

The church's explosive growth was fueled by the teaching of a three-fold blessing enjoyed by followers of Jesus Christ, blessings to the body, soul, and spirit, including financial prosperity. Pastor Cho also emphasized mid-week cell group meetings, often led by women, which went against the grain of Korean culture. The cell groups included Bible study, worship, and prayer. There was always an assistant leader in training, so when the group reached a certain size, the cell divided.

After outgrowing one facility, the church purchased a plot of land on an island in the middle of the Han River, which winds its way through the heart of Seoul, directly across from the National Assembly. Even though they built a facility that held 12,000, they maxed the capacity with seven Sunday services by 1983 and were forced to develop satellite locations throughout the city.

By the time of our visit with their team, Pastor Cho's

church had been recognized as the largest in the world, with several hundred thousand attending on Sunday mornings. Their foundation was cell groups, and J.P. wanted to go see how they did it.

Unfortunately, in the week following our wedding and only days before our trip, we were involved in an auto accident on Pacific Coast Highway in Dana Point near the Harbor House restaurant. It was not unusual for J.P. to have accidents. The fact that I was in the car is what was unusual. He was making a lefthand turn, and a car hit us at forty miles an hour. We jumped the curb and almost went into the Killer Dana Surf Shop. J.P. fell on top of me.

J.P. wasn't wearing his seat belt. The highway patrolman said he would have been killed if he would have had it on. The car hit the driver's door and knocked him over, and he wound up on my lap.

Thankfully, there were no serious, life-threatening injuries, but I suffered a very badly sprained ankle. I had never traveled overseas, and I wanted to go. We got on the plane and went. I bandaged my ankle and hobbled along. Sometimes I could hardly wear a shoe because of the swelling.

Before our arrival, Pastor Homer Waisner encouraged each team member to inquire of the Lord about an area of their life that needed healing. The church in Korea had an area called Prayer Mountain. People would go up there and pray and get answers from God. I asked God to show me healing is real so I would strengthen my faith and believe He heals.

Established in 1973 on a wooded hill north of the church near the DMZ, Prayer Mountain is a retreat destination for one million visitors a year who are focused on intensive prayer and fasting. Shuttle buses run between the main church and Prayer Mountain all day, every day, 365 days a year.

When we arrived at Prayer Mountain, I found it painfully difficult to manage the hundreds of steps to get to the massive chapel. I continued praying God would help me with my lack of faith in healing. I had never been healed of anything in my life.

We finally sat down in the chapel and put on our headphones for translation as the service began. The man leading the service said, "I feel the Spirit of God in this room. I want you to pray with me, and we're going to see God at work. If you have an illness or something wrong, touch the place where it hurts you." Then he began praying in tongues and invited others to join with him in prayer.

J.P. was struck by the sound of so many people praying together. He said it was the most incredible sound he'd ever heard. There were people from all over the world praying at the same time. It sounded like a peaceful, babbling brook. It wasn't loud. It was sweet. Some were joining in with tongues.

In response to the pastor's instructions, I reached down and touched my right ankle, which was incredibly swollen. All of a sudden, my ankle was hot, like it was on fire. Something kept twirling and twirling and twirling in my ankle bone.

I wondered what was going on. I didn't say anything to my husband or anybody there. All of a sudden, I felt a pop in my ankle bone, the swelling went down, and my ankle was completely normal. I was sitting there in awe. The pastor didn't touch me. Nobody said my name. It just happened.

I was miraculously healed by the Lord's touch! When the service finished, we went down the stairs, and I felt no pain. My ankle was normal. I knew for sure I was healed when I got out in the sunlight and could see I was able to walk down the stairs.

During our time at the Yoido church, Rev. Robert

Schuller happened to be visiting at the same time and was invited on stage. J.P. knew that Schuller liked Dr. Cho, but in the middle of the service with Schuller on stage, Dr. Cho asked him to leave. He could sense he was not authentic.

During our first year of marriage, we also went on a mission trip to Kenya for three weeks. We did evangelistic street preaching in a little town called Meru. When you go to a third-world country, you can guarantee some people will get sick. We were in this one service, and I was not feeling well, vomiting. I said I wanted to return to our hotel room until I felt better.

While we stayed at the nicest hotel in Meru, our room happened to be situated above a bar. I could hear prostitutes getting beat up below us, and my pillow felt like it was made out of knotted rags. Our room also lacked hot water.

When J.P. returned to the room to check on my condition, he expected to find me in a dejected, woeful state of mind. Instead, he was pleasantly surprised to see me full of thanksgiving. I told him I was so grateful I was born in America and didn't have a terminal illness.

J.P. marveled at my attitude. I didn't feel well, but I was still so grateful. J.P. believed that was the start of a turning point in my life with God.

After I left Mariners Church, I landed a job working for Fieldstone Company in Newport Beach, California. I had a really good job selling new homes. I told my boss, Peter Ochs, that I wanted to be a pastor's wife and didn't want to work on Sundays anymore so I could go with my husband to church. Peter, a strong Christian, understood. He was a gentleman.

Chapter 8

Learning to Forgive

When it came time to sell the first home we bought together in Laguna Niguel, the buyer could not afford to purchase the house outright. As part of the offer, the buyer asked us to carry a second trust deed of $80,000.

We agreed to the deal and moved out of the house. The buyer owned a limo service and had a boat at Dana Point Harbor. His wife owned a beauty salon. In time we got a notice they had not made any house payments on the first trust deed. We didn't know they weren't making payments. We finally got a letter from the holder of the first saying it was in foreclosure.

Angry about the situation we found ourselves in, we met with the other couple. "What's going on?" J.P. demanded. "Why didn't you tell us? Now we're going to lose the house!"

The real estate market at that time wasn't strong, and the property had not appreciated. It wasn't worth it for us to put out the $80,000.

I was upset and had difficulty with the idea of taking the loss, much less forgiving the other couple. We lost our money, everything we initially invested in the home. I was very angry with them. My husband processed it in such a way that he told them he forgave them.

The home we moved into was only a short distance away, so we faced the likely possibility of running into them after the default. We committed that whenever we saw them, we would go up to them and ask how they were doing. We would try to act as normally as possible and never bring up the money loss. That was the beginning for me of learning how to forgive. I found it harder to forgive than J.P. did. He is a very forgiving person. I have to process it with God for a while.

One day we came out of a bagel shop in Laguna Niguel and spied the other couple. "There are Sarah and her husband," J.P. said. "Let's see how they're doing."

As soon as the other couple saw us, they turned around quickly and walked the other way. They left—they bolted!

Our conscience was clear; we had forgiven them. For God spoke to us and said to count it as joy when we go through various trials (James 1:2). It was a very difficult thing to do, but we obeyed God and felt a new freedom.

...

A few months later, a neighbor named Larry came to J.P. and asked if he could borrow $10,000. It was tax money we set aside, and I was adamantly against it. He said he would pay us back in a week and I said no, no, no because J.P. could lose the friendship they had developed if Larry did not pay us back.

By every indication Larry was successful in sales, had a boat at the harbor, and drove a Mercedes. Larry and J.P. served on the board of a Christian charity together. He told J.P. he would give him his boat as collateral. He said he had a big deal closing soon and could pay us back the next week.

The big deal never closed. Three months later, J.P. knocked on his door and asked, "What's going on? Why didn't you pay me back?"

Larry launched into a halting explanation about why he couldn't repay the $10,000.

"I am going to have your boat, right?" J.P. asked.

"Oh no, you can't have my boat," Larry replied. He

reminded J.P. there wasn't any contract. They only had a handshake and verbal agreement.

J.P. was understandably upset by the betrayal of trust by someone who professed to be a believer. He was our Christian brother, friend, and member of our board. Incredibly, Larry and his wife began leading a church group that dealt with Christian financial stewardship. Someone in the group confronted them about not repaying us, accusing them of being hypocrites. His wife said it was unfair we wanted our money back. As a result of the situation, everyone quit going to the group.

Larry also happened to serve as a police chaplain. The police department called us because Larry was asking for money from some of the policemen driving him around. Then a pastor in Laguna Beach called us up and said Larry wanted to be an elder. He heard through the grapevine that he owed us money.

"I understand he owes you $10,000. Is that correct?" the pastor asked.

"Yes," J.P. replied.

"Has that created a hardship for you?"

"No, God has blessed me, and I believe one of the reasons he has blessed me is because I've forgiven him. I just bought a new Toyota pickup and paid cash."

Chapter 9

Launching a Ministry

We started La Tienda Thrift Store in Capistrano Beach shortly after we were married. We rented a house across the street and took in men with alcohol and drug problems. The thrift store supported the house. We had to sell one of our cars to put the down payment on the store.

We had a real challenge the first year we started the ministry. We put up all the money for leasing the building, got it opened, and started the nonprofit. We also opened up a food bank in San Juan Capistrano.

A prominent businessman had started a free medical clinic nearby. He called us because he wanted to find out more about our plans, so we met in his office. He peppered us with questions, concluding we were meeting the same needs. "You are meeting practical needs, and I'm meeting physical needs," said the businessman.

J.P. explained how we planned to run the thrift store, and it sparked the businessman's interest. "Maybe we could even open up a thrift store together," he told J.P.

We left the man's office, soaring in the clouds thinking God had provided a significant financial backer for our ministry. "We just got funded!" J.P. exulted.

A few weeks later, we met with Barbara, the administrator for the businessman who ran the free clinic. She began to dig deeper, asking more probing questions. "If people come for food, do you pray with them?" she asked. "What would happen if a woman came in, and she was pregnant? What would you tell her?"

"We tell her we would love to have her keep the baby— anything we could do to save the baby," J.P. replied.

"We are neutral," the woman said frostily. J.P. shot a glance at the businessman, who was quiet. His face was set like flint, which surprised J.P.

J.P. looked at me, and I looked back at him. "Look, this is a bottom line," J.P. said. "We are unashamedly evangelical Christians. We believe abortion is murder and would do anything we could do to save that baby."

"We are neutral," the woman repeated. "We wouldn't say anything for or against an abortion."

We never heard from the businessman or his administrator again. I think he thought this could be a can of worms and cause problems in their building with the staff because he had some doctors in there donating time. But we walked out of there and said we will always put God first and do what He tells us to do. God provided for us every step of the way. This was laying the groundwork for other donors to come around.

J.P.'s close friend and handball partner, Fred, managed the thrift store. He was able to volunteer because his wife received a generous income from a family trust.

After building up a successful ministry, disaster struck. We lost the lease on the store after it expired. Fred went behind our backs and signed a three-year lease on a smaller space in the same shopping center. That was the hardest thing J.P. ever went through with a person because Fred was his best friend. He took the trucks we used for the ministry, everything. One day we were getting money from the store, and the next day we were done.

It seems Fred convinced J.P. to sign a contract that transferred ownership of the thrift store to Fred. J.P. hadn't protected himself in any way. He didn't think he had to because Fred was his best friend.

"If someone asks, 'What are these wounds on your body?' they will answer, 'The wounds

I was given at the house of my friends.'" (Zechariah 13:6 NIV)

Shortly after that, J.P. confronted Fred. "Fred, I'm so devastated. When did that truck become your truck? When did all the receipts from the store become yours?"

"If I have my name on this, I can give more to the ministry," Fred replied.

Fred's explanation and the perception of another betrayal of trust was a big hurdle for J.P. After our pastor preached a sermon about forgiveness, J.P. asked to meet with Fred in the pastor's office. The pastor forewarned J.P. it would be a hard meeting.

Pastor Roger opened the meeting and said, "J.P., would you like to speak first?"

"Yes," he said. "Fred, when did that store become yours?"

Fred sat in his chair with a glum expression on his face. "I have nothing to say," he retorted, and his lip began quivering.

J.P., moved with compassion, began to cry. Then he went over to his friend and said, "Fred, I want to bless you with the thrift store."

At that moment—when J.P. chose to extend grace and forgive his friend—he says he was set free.

Now J.P. and Fred are close friends, closer than they have ever been, and they can joke about the situation. His wife died and left him with three kids. J.P.'s wife died and left him with three kids. They had gone through a lot together. It could have been an absolute disaster for J.P. if he had held onto that bitterness. After that, Fred gave a large amount to support our ministry.

•••

Three years after Larry stiffed us on the $10,000 loan, he walked into the men's home in Capistrano Beach, bawling like a baby. He was driving an old Ford Maverick. He said, "J.P., I'm so sorry. Will you forgive me?"

J.P. said yes and marveled at the way God worked all things together for good. We became friends with Larry and got back to where we had fellowship. His wife, an interior decorator, owned a commercial building in Oregon. She loved to buy stuff and do some decorating. She couldn't sell the stuff but had to pay for storage. She leased numerous storage facilities but got behind on her rent. She said to us, "If you will come and pick the items up, you can have them."

J.P. went and picked them up. He did that five times. The storage units contained nice decorative items, furniture, and clothes. We were able to sell all of it and get back more than the $10,000 Larry owed us. We just sold the last of what she had, an old door. It sold for $1200. God worked it all out, and J.P. and Larry have a good relationship.

...

> Then Peter came to Him and said, "Lord, how often shall my brother sin against me, and I forgive him? Up to seven times?"
>
> Jesus said to him, "I do not say to you, up to seven times, but up to seventy times seven. Therefore the kingdom of heaven is like a certain king who wanted to settle accounts with his servants. And when he had begun to settle accounts, one was brought to him who owed him ten thousand talents. But as he was not able to pay, his master commanded that he be sold, with his wife and children and all that he had, and that payment be made. The servant therefore fell down before him, saying, 'Master, have patience with me, and I will pay you all.' Then the master of that servant was moved with compassion, released him, and forgave him the debt.

"But that servant went out and found one of his fellow servants who owed him a hundred denarii; and he laid hands on him and took him by the throat, saying, 'Pay me what you owe!' So his fellow servant fell down at his feet and begged him, saying, 'Have patience with me, and I will pay you all.' And he would not, but went and threw him into prison till he should pay the debt. So when his fellow servants saw what had been done, they were very grieved, and came and told their master all that had been done. Then his master, after he had called him, said to him, 'You wicked servant! I forgave you all that debt because you begged me. Should you not also have had compassion on your fellow servant, just as I had pity on you?' And his master was angry, and delivered him to the torturers until he should pay all that was due to him.

"So My heavenly Father also will do to you if each of you, from his heart, does not forgive his brother his trespasses." (Matthew 18:21–35)

CRACKED VESSELS

Chapter 10

Taking in a Troubled Young Man

J.P. had only been a Christian for a few months when he was asked to preach at Believer's Chapel in San Clemente, which had no pastor but was started by a graduate of Dallas Theological Seminary. The church was run by seven elders.

He was very zealous when he gave his first sermon. Most of the church was away at a couples' retreat, but he didn't go because Saturday was his big day in the barbershop.

Hardly anyone was at church that morning—hardly any unsaved people there. Usually, everybody knew everybody who was there, and they were all Christians. He preached the gospel and asked if anybody wanted to receive Jesus, they should raise their hands. He had his eyes closed and didn't look up because he wasn't expecting anybody to get saved.

However, a young couple, Katherine and her husband were visiting the church that morning, and they were powerfully moved by the preaching of the Word and by the Spirit. They raised their hands to receive Jesus in response to J.P.'s invitation and were born again.

The next Sunday, they came to church and told somebody about their new faith. J.P. met them for the first time, and over the next few years, they became close friends with J.P. and me.

However, their growth in the Lord was challenged by a rebellious teenager at home. They had a fourteen-year-old son who was a wild kid and no one appeared to tolerate his attitude.

We had started a sixty-day drug recovery program

ranch at Lake Elsinore on five acres. Thirty to forty men were living at the ranch at that time in mobile homes, and Gary, their son, had been persuaded to enter the program in his mid-twenties. After his first week at the ranch, his recovery was not going well. Gary had become a disruptive influence on the other men.

When it became apparent it was not working, J.P. sat down with him and delivered some straight talk. "Gary, how does it feel to be the biggest asshole at this ranch, and nobody likes you?"

Gary fidgeted in his chair, his eyes blazing in defiant indifference. "You can't stay here," J.P. continued. "You want to fight with everybody. What am I going to do with you?"

J.P. shook his head in exasperation, then did something few people would do. He asked Gary to come and live in our own home. J.P. told him he had no choice because Gary's mom and dad were his friends, and they kicked him out ... so he had to come live with us.

This unusual extension of grace brought surprising results. We grew to love and support him. One day I sat down with Gary and told him he needed to be on medication. He was off drugs but needed meds. I could tell he was bipolar or ADHD. I told him being on some meds would allow him to have a better life.

We paid for his first appointment with a doctor in San Clemente. In his first month of medication after being diagnosed, Gary's life turned around because he began to follow Christ, overcame his addiction, and found medical help. These changes led to him meeting a wonderful young lady named Katy, who became his wife.

•••

Twenty years later we got an unexpected call from Gary. He had a wonderful wife and family, but he slipped and started drinking, so he called us. His wife threatened to remove him from the house. He called us in desperation. After we hung up, I told J.P. we had to call him back and let him stay with us. So he came.

Gary stayed as a guest in our home for a week. We didn't go anywhere, not even out to eat.

We didn't tell him what to do. All we did was sit and listen to him talk. We loved on him without judging him and prayed for his healing.

He told us about being abused as a child by a relative. People didn't know about this. He told us so many things. He wept and got so much off his chest. When he left, he was a different man.

He is accountable to J.P. and calls him every morning. He says he's fixing up a bedroom for us to come and stay as long as we want. He even has a house he is working on, and when the renter passes, he wants us to live there on his property. We told him we can't do that, but we will come and visit. Gary and Katy just celebrated their eleventh wedding anniversary and have two wonderful children.

Three elements are critical: forgiveness, love, and a non-judgmental attitude. That's what God has taught us over the years, to love others and to forgive, without judgment.

CRACKED VESSELS

Chapter 11

Beans, Rice, and Jesus Christ

The men who pass through the men's ranch often have colorful stories about their lives. One such man, Jake, was no exception. He told me his father was president of Anheuser-Busch, and he had been working in real estate. He said he spent some time in prison because he had taken advantage of the elderly.

He kept telling J.P. he was going to build him a ranch, better than the ranch he had. He was living with us in our home on Ortega Hwy near Lake Elsinore. J.P. started feeling he was delusional. He also told J.P. he owned the Arco Tower. It was just one thing after another.

J.P. decided to challenge Jake one day. "Why don't you buy me a house?" J.P. asked him.

"I have to graduate first from the program," Jake muttered.

Jake was currently enrolled in a one-year rehab program. Then he started working in a thrift store owned by us at an outlet mall in Lake Elsinore. The thrift store helped support the ministry.

He was taking money out of the till. He also had a girlfriend, and she would back up her car to the store and load it with decorator items. They would sell the merchandise they were stealing.

Jake's friend (also living with us) got drunk one night and began to wallow in remorse. He knew about Jake's thieving and decided to come clean. He called J.P. and said he couldn't take it anymore. He said, "Jake has been stealing all along, giving money out of the till to his girlfriend, and I had to tell you."

The next day, J.P. drove to the thrift store and confronted Jake: "You've been stealing from the ministry!"

Jake hung his head down and confessed to his wrongdoing. "Don't turn me into the police," he begged. "Send me to Cabazon."

We were affiliated with another rehab ranch operated by Set Free Ministries located in Cabazon, an unincorporated area best known for its giant dinosaur statues visible from Interstate 10, a massive outlet mall, and the Morongo casino. But hidden away from the freeway traffic was a spartan, dirt-bare ranch with two aged mobile homes sitting on it.

Cabazon, a real primitive place, was the purgatory of our whole ministry. The record was 123 men housed in two mobile homes with wall-to-wall bunks. They would also sleep outside on the ground waiting to get in. It was beans and rice and Jesus Christ. Most of the camp was outside.

J.P. turned to Jake and said, "I guess I can take you to Cabazon, but first, I have to take you to our house to get your stuff."

When they went into his room, J.P. discovered Jake had also stolen several pieces of my jewelry and had been hiding them in a bag.

After J.P. dropped him in Cabazon, he happened to run into Jake's ex-wife a few months later.

"Tell me about Jake. He's told me a lot of stories. I'm not sure how much is true," he began.

"His father was a janitor at Hughes Aircraft and never owned a home," she explained. "Jake was a petty thief, a kleptomaniac—not a white-collar criminal. Because of that, he spent some time in jail, but he never went to prison. We had kids together, but he couldn't support any of us because he couldn't keep a job."

J.P. shakes his head as he considers all the men who

have passed through the doors of the ministry—many with tales of woe from challenging circumstances in their past, and many nursing more than their share of self-inflicted wounds. J.P. never heard from Jake again. He left the ranch and never showed up wanting to get back in.

We try to never give up on anybody, we forgive everybody, and give everybody a second chance. That's the real story.

CRACKED VESSELS

Chapter 12
Jenna's Struggle

God did a mighty miracle in Jenna, J.P. and Carol's daughter, by restoring her eyesight as a baby. As Jenna's life unfolded, however, she dealt with a series of heavy challenges.

In her thirties, Jenna developed Guillain–Barré syndrome, which involved muscle weakness that began in her hands and feet and gradually spread throughout her upper body. It is considered an autoimmune disorder, wherein the sufferer's immune system mistakenly attacks the myelin insulation of the nervous system. As the disease progresses, it can be life-threatening, with changes to the heart rate and blood pressure. Some people require mechanical ventilation. The death rate globally from the syndrome is about 7.5 percent.

Jenna was in the hospital for almost two months, and she was in a coma at one time. First, she had trouble walking. Her legs just died, and she became paralyzed. She started to lose the ability to talk. She couldn't see and was intubated.

We prayed fervently for her recovery, and remarkably, she improved enough to be released from the hospital.

Jenna's husband, Bill, was not a believer. Jenna had problems in her marriage due to her deteriorating health and other relational issues exacerbated by an addiction to prescription meds and alcohol. Jenna was a real sweetheart when she was sober, but she wasn't sober a lot, and she was bipolar.

Bill was very much against what we believed as Christians. They both drank a lot. Bill was always leaving her but would come back within a few days. Police had to come to the home because the neighbors complained about screaming and fighting.

The pattern kept repeating itself until Bill left for a more extended period. Jenna feared the worst. After she'd been alone for two weeks, Jenna called her dad and said Bill left her. "Oh, he does that a lot," J.P. replied. "He'll be back in a few days, don't worry."

Jenna called J.P. almost every night to say Bill was still gone and tell him how depressed she was.

"We will keep praying, and he should come back," J.P. encouraged her.

One evening J.P. turned to me and said, "You know, I'm a little worried about Jenna. She hasn't called me. It's been almost a week. We were talking almost daily."

"You know Jenna, she'll be calling you. Don't worry," I said. "Maybe Bill's come back, and she's fine."

Two days later J.P. was at the hardware store and got a phone call from Bill. "Jenna is dead! Jenna is dead!" he sobbed into the phone. "Why didn't you take care of her? It's your fault she died." Then he unleashed a volley of horrible curses at J.P.

The dreaded news—along with the accusation—hit J.P. like a sledgehammer. J.P. was so stunned, he just started driving around and couldn't even get home. Jenna was only thirty-nine when she passed.

Still despondent, J.P. finally called me on the phone, but he was so hysterical I couldn't comprehend him.

"What's the matter? What's the matter? I can't understand what you're saying," I said.

"Jenna's dead! Jenna's dead. Bill called me and said it was my fault she died and why didn't I take care of her. Bill was crying. He's so sad. He's crying and crying. And he called me horrible names."

"Just come home," I said.

The next day J.P. called Bill to ask about funeral arrangements. "Where is her body?" J.P. asked.

"You're not going to see her," Bill replied. "She's at the coroner's. Since it was a suspicious death, they're doing an autopsy. I'm next of kin, and you're not getting near her."

After that, our phone calls to Bill went unanswered. We held a memorial service for Jenna at Heritage Church in San Clemente. Bill was invited but never showed up. None of the family ever saw her body, and I guess in some ways that was God's grace.

It seems Jenna had been dead for two days before she was found. She had a dog that she adored, and the dog had been barking for two days. The neighbors said that wasn't like her dog, and something was wrong. They knocked on the door, but nobody responded. So, they called the authorities to ask for a welfare check.

A family member called the coroner's office and learned Jenna died from an overdose of drugs and alcohol, which they believe was accidental. She was terrified of dying. We surmise she accidentally drank too much and took some pills, not realizing how much she was taking.

A year after Jenna's death, we returned home from a short vacation. When we returned to church, Pastor Roger Gales took us aside and said, "Your son-in-law Bill has been looking for you."

J.P. called him immediately, feeling some trepidation because of Bill's prior treatment. Bill informed J.P. he had been diagnosed with throat cancer. Since the diagnosis, he had been attending a cancer recovery group at J.P.'s church.

When J.P. went to meet with Bill, he was surprised by the change in his demeanor and countenance. He was very, very nice. He wasn't drinking because of the cancer.

Then came the amazing news: "I've received Jesus as my Savior and Lord!" he told J.P.

At one of the recovery meetings, Bill finally surrendered his life to Jesus Christ. We totally forgave him, and he apologized for hiding Jenna from us. We offered to let Bill stay at our home while he recovered from cancer. "Please come and stay with us. We'll take care of you," we told him.

"No, no, I'm much better, I'll be fine," he replied, perhaps carrying a measure of remorse over the way he treated us in the past.

J.P. thought he had a lot of guilt, but we didn't carry any hard feelings about what he did.

Later Bill formed a nonprofit to help other cancer patients by driving them to chemotherapy, cleaning their homes, mowing their lawns, and shopping for them—all the things a person can't do when struggling with a debilitating disease.

When Bill asked J.P.'s advice about raising money for his ministry, J.P. told him not to focus on fundraising. The money would come in when he was doing the stuff.

A few weeks later Bill called J.P. and said, "My God, you were right. I did the stuff. I picked up a lady who had cancer, and it just happened to be throat cancer. I took her to chemotherapy and then stopped at the grocery store, bought her some groceries, and took her home. It was the best experience I ever had in my life!"

After a couple of months went by, J.P. had an opportunity to preach, and he talked about losing Jenna. He said, "Here's my thought on God's character ... for God so loved Jenna, He allowed her—He could have stopped it—but allowed her to come home and be with Him because she knew the Lord, and she would be in a place where *'God will wipe away every tear from their eyes; there shall be no more death, nor sorrow, nor crying.*

There shall be no more pain, for the former things have passed away'" (Revelation 21:4).

CRACKED VESSELS

Chapter 13

An Eleventh-Hour Prayer

One of the elders at Ocean Hills Church, Bob Fraunzimmer, had a dad named Max who moved to Southern California from New Jersey. When Max asked his son about finding a barber in the area, he recommended J.P.

One day Max walked into the barbershop and announced to J.P., "I'm Bob's dad, and you're going to be my barber."

J.P. learned that in New Jersey, you pick a barber and stay with him. Nobody else cut Max's hair but him. People were not as loyal in Southern California, but that was the practice back there.

As was his habit, J.P. witnessed to Max about his faith the first time he was in the chair.

"I don't believe that stuff," Max huffed.

J.P. cut Max's hair for quite a few years, but then Max stopped coming in. He got cancer and got very sick. Bob called him up one day and said, "I don't think my dad will make it through the night. Could you come to see him?"

After J.P. rushed to San Clemente Hospital, he entered Max's room and went to his bedside but couldn't wake him up. Discouraged, J.P. left Max's room, went to the lobby, and called Bob.

"I'm sorry. I can't wake your dad," J.P. said.

Because J.P.'s car was parked behind the hospital, he walked down the long hallway toward Max's room and decided to make one last attempt to communicate with him.

J.P. went to his bedside and bent over so that his face was close to Max's head. "Max, you're at the gate. Will you repent and receive Jesus as your Savior?"

J.P. was startled when Max opened his eyes and looked at him directly. "Yes!" Max said, his soul dangling by a slender strand on this side of eternity. Then he passed.

J.P. saw how God is so gracious, saving His children in their final moments.

...

A woman named Barbara attended at Ocean Hills Church where J.P. pastored. Her father, Frank, owned Frank Beck's Garage Door Repair. He was being treated for cancer at the City of Hope in downtown L.A.

Barbara wanted J.P. to talk to her dad, so he went down to the City of Hope. He was hopeful as he entered Frank's room and sat down in a chair near his bed. After some small talk, J.P. presented the gospel to Frank.

"I don't believe that crap," Frank told J.P. "Get out of my room!"

Disheartened, J.P. left the hospital. Frank was gruff, one of the gruffest ones.

A few weeks later was J.P.'s birthday, and I had invited some friends over to watch a Mike Tyson fight on TV. As we prepared for our friends to arrive, J.P. got a desperate call from Barbara. Doctors had given up on Frank and sent him home, saying they could do nothing more for him.

"J.P., my dad won't wake up. Can you come over?"

Immediately, J.P. left the house and drove to Barbara's. When J.P. entered the room, he found her crying next to her father. She was sitting, straddling her dad, holding his head in her hands and sobbing.

J.P. recognized Frank's time was short. He approached them and said, "Frank, Frank, you're getting close to the gate, buddy. Will you repent?"

Frank slowly opened his eyes, summoned his remaining strength, and said, "Yes."

"Will you receive Jesus as your Savior?" J.P. asked.

"Yes," Frank replied with more conviction.

"Did you ask Jesus into your heart?"

"Yes!!!" Frank yelled out, and then he died.

Jesus said, *"Behold, I stand at the door and knock. If anyone hears My voice and opens the door, I will come in to him and dine with him, and he with Me"* (Revelation 3:20).

The man who repaired doors for most of his life kept the door to his heart shut until the final minutes of his life on earth. Then he said yes to Jesus, left Barbara's arms, and entered into the embrace of his Savior, to enjoy His presence forever.

Chapter 14

Charlie's Funeral

For a brief period, J.P. was the pastor of a Calvary Chapel church in Bothell, Washington, a northern suburb of Seattle near Lake Washington.

J.P. was new on the job. A lady whose husband died called. She wanted somebody to do the funeral. He jumped on it. He loved to do funerals because he loved to share the good news about Jesus Christ.

After agreeing to officiate, J.P. learned that neither the husband, Charlie, nor his wife was a Christian. Charlie had been president of the most prominent bank in the community.

J.P. visited the wife and their son, Charlie Jr., to go over the arrangements. "Do you want to speak at the funeral?" J.P. asked her.

"No, I couldn't eulogize him," she said.

J.P. turned to the son and asked him the same question. "I haven't spoken to my dad in five years," he said. "I can't do it."

J.P. learned the father and son had been estranged for quite a while. Charlie's sister and daughter also declined to speak.

"Well, since I didn't know him, it would be better if you had somebody who could eulogize him. Is there anyone?" J.P. asked.

The daughter suggested a former neighbor named Harold, who had once been the family dentist.

J.P. got Harold's phone number and called him the next day. "Will you speak at Charlie's funeral?" J.P. asked.

"Well, I've never done anything like that. I don't know if I could do it, but I guess if no one else is available, I could probably say a few words," he said.

"Okay, could you get there early? I will go through what I'm going to do. First, I'll welcome people and read a psalm or something, then I'll call you up. Does that sound okay?" he asked.

"Yes, yes, that sounds fine," Harold said.

On the appointed day, J.P. arrived early but couldn't find Harold. He didn't come early. J.P. didn't see him and didn't even know if he was there when he started ... J.P. started a little late, thinking he might come, but didn't even know what he looked like.

More than 500 had turned out for the memorial, partly because Charlie was born and raised in Bothell and had become a well-regarded member of the community.

When the moment arrived for the eulogy, J.P. asked the crowd, "Excuse me, but is Harold here?"

Harold slowly stood up and ambled forward toward the open casket. He appeared to be somewhat feeble and didn't have any notes with him.

"Well, I've known Charlie for fifty-two years or something like that," Harold began. "He was my next-door neighbor. Charlie was kind of stubborn ... he was the president of the bank, born here in this town."

Harold approached the open casket, touched the edge, and glanced inside. Then he began to address the corpse as if Charlie could still hear. "Charlie, do you remember the night when I just moved in, and you and your wife invited us over to your house for dinner? Do you remember I shared the gospel with you?"

"You said you weren't interested," Harold continued. "Charlie, do you remember when you beat that other neighbor up? Charlie, Charlie, it's too late, Charlie. Oh, how I wished you would have listened, but it's too late for you!"

Filled with emotion, Harold broke down and began to sob. He turned from the casket and began to shuffle back to his seat in the pew. Before he sat down, something else came to his mind and he turned toward the family: "Charlie Jr., you're just like him. You're going down the same road that he went down, drinking and fighting ..."

Choked up, Harold couldn't say anything more and sat down.

J.P. paused for a moment to reflect on the gravity of Harold's words and then said, "I'd like to allow you to hear the gospel. The gospel has four parts. God loves you, but you messed it up. Charlie messed it up big time. But Jesus came to fix it. You need to repent, turn away from your sins, and receive Jesus as your Savior and Lord. I'm going to open up this altar here and ask if anyone wants to receive Jesus as their Savior, just come forward."

The first person to stand up was Charlie Jr.!

People followed his lead and began to stand up all over the church. J.P. would say at least 100 people came forward. It was amazing. He didn't do anything but give them the gospel. It was so incredibly amazing.

"For I am not ashamed of the gospel of Christ, for it is the power of God to salvation for everyone who believes, for the Jew first and also for the Greek." (Romans 1:16)

CRACKED VESSELS

Chapter 15

Ministry Life

When J.P. served as senior associate pastor at Ocean Hills Church, I was managing several salespeople for a homebuilder in Orange County.

One day a salesperson in the office told me, "I just sold the house next door to you to a gay couple."

When I informed J.P. later that day, he was upset. "You've got to nix that deal," he said.

"I'm not going to nix that deal," I retorted.

"Well, they're going to have parties and all kinds of stuff ... and we have a Bible study at our house every Monday night," he protested.

"Honey, you can't be prejudiced as a Christian. It would be best if you went to meet him," I said.

J.P. did not go over immediately to meet our new neighbors. A few weeks went by, and J.P. started a project to landscape our new house. He decided he would propose to the new neighbors that we all share the cost of planting a tree on the boundary line between the two houses since only eight or ten feet were separating them.

J.P. knocked on the neighbor's front door, introduced himself, and found out the man at the door was named Rob. "It's too small to have your landscaping and my landscaping," J.P. told him. "Why don't we pick out a tree together, and we can go in on it half and half."

Rob agreed to the plan. But after the landscaping was completed, Rob never reimbursed us for his half of the cost, which annoyed J.P.

Another man was living with Rob, but apparently, they split up, because the other man stopped coming around. Then we noticed a nurse would come by Rob's house and leave something on the doorstep. "I think he's got AIDS," J.P. told me.

It was in the early stage of the disease when there was much hysteria among the general public about HIV/AIDS, especially after actor Rock Hudson announced he had AIDS and died three months later. There were no effective treatments, and for many, contracting the disease represented a death sentence. Having AIDS had a stigma attached to it, and there were numerous misconceptions about how the disease was transmitted. Some falsely believed the disease could be passed through casual contact.

One day J.P. was driving to church, and God convicted him about his attitude toward Rob. When he reached the church, he sat down at his desk but felt the overwhelming sense he should leave the church and meet with Rob immediately.

J.P. drove home and knocked on the front door of Rob's house. Rob opened the door about three inches. "Can I come in?" J.P. inquired.

"Yes," Rob replied, somewhat cautiously.

They sat down on the couch together, and then J.P. did something many might not have done at the time. He put his hand on Rob's knee and asked, "Do you have AIDS?"

Rob's lower lip started quivering, and his eyes welled up with tears. "Yes," he said quietly.

"I'm so sorry ... How can I help you?" J.P. asked.

Rob thought for a moment. "You could mow my lawn for me," he ventured. He was already too weak to complete the chore, something he had done easily before he got sick and lost his strength. "And I need a haircut ..."

Rob had no way of knowing J.P.'s professional background. "I used to be a barber," J.P. said. "Yes, I can cut your hair."

After dinner several nights a week, J.P. would walk next door and sit with Rob. He found out he was completely estranged from his dad, and they hadn't spoken in years. He got weaker and weaker. One night J.P. shared the gospel with him and led him to Jesus. And he became a different person. Whenever it was time for J.P. to return home in the evening, Rob would give him a thumbs up.

Finally, the time came when Rob was too weak to walk up the stairs to his bedroom, so J.P.'s son, Paul, would carry him upstairs. When he got closer to the end, J.P. called Rob's dad, who came and reconciled with Rob.

Then Rob was transferred to a hospice in Laguna Beach. So J.P. went down there and told them he was his pastor, but the staff wouldn't let him in. The last time J.P. saw him, he put his thumbs up.

J.P. officiated the memorial service for Rob in his house. Many gay people came, and so many people were reconciled at that service. It ended well, and Rob went to be with the Lord. There is no question in J.P.'s mind that Rob went to heaven.

Chapter 16

Children Belong to God

When I was selling homes at a tract in Rancho Santa Margarita, one of the women who worked for the company came into the office very distraught. I learned an employee at a local business park shot his three children and killed himself. One of the children was in critical condition in the hospital.

According to news accounts, the husband, upset over a custody dispute involving his children, shot and killed his nine-year-old son, wounded his two younger sons, and then fatally shot himself at a building in the Rancho Santa Margarita Business Park.

The father and nine-year-old son were declared dead at the scene. The two surviving sons, ages three and five, were taken to Mission Community Hospital in Mission Viejo.

In the divorce proceedings, the wife alleged that her husband had a five-year history of physically and emotionally abusing her. The couple had also been in and out of court-ordered counseling during the months leading up to the shootings, according to media stories.

As soon as I heard about the tragedy, I called J.P. and said, "J.P., you have to go to the hospital. There's this woman, and she's the mother of three little boys. The father took the children into a shed, and he shot all three of them, but one they thought might survive. He shot them and then shot himself because he didn't want his wife to take the boys. Selfishly, he wanted to kill everybody ..."

At this point in our lives, if I saw something in the newspaper, and some people needed help or needed a word of encouragement from a pastor, I would call J.P. and ask him if he would respond.

"Do you have the time? Can you go over there?" I would ask.

And J.P. would always say, "Of course, yes!"

He rushed to Mission Hospital and met with the wife. She didn't have any family nearby. So J.P. prayed with her and called her every day.

The nine-year-old son who died had played on a Little League baseball team as the second baseman. We had a memorial service at the baseball field, and the whole team came.

J.P. invited a band called The Dime-a-Dozen to play. One of the songs they sung at that emotion-filled service was "Gathering Flowers for the Master's Bouquet." Its lyrics—perfect for the occasion—describe a person who has died as now residing in heaven forever to bloom in the Lord's presence.

J.P. shared the gospel, and some people raised their hands. What he remembers is the shortstop on the Little League team. He was probably nine or ten, and his mother brought him to me. He was crying because he didn't share the gospel with the boy that died.

J.P. assured the boy that children who die before a certain age go straight to heaven. He told him that in the Bible when David lost a child, he said, *"I shall go to him, but he shall not return to me"* (2 Samuel 12:23).

J.P. prayed with him, and it was so heartwarming because this little boy had a heart for where his buddy was going to spend eternity. And so, despite the tragedy, the service was a victorious one in that people were saved, and this little boy got touched. J.P. wishes he knew where that little shortstop was today.

Chapter 17

No God Wanted

Funeral services was what J.P. liked doing best—particularly for families who were not Christians—and made arrangements with the owner of Lesneski's Mortuary in San Clemente to officiate any services when the family did not have a pastor available. He would go visit the family and ask them what they would like to do. Sometimes a family member would say they didn't want a "churchy" funeral.

"Well, you know I'm a Christian," J.P. would reply, "so I gotta say something. I'll read a psalm and pray a prayer." And that's what he would do.

After everyone shared, J.P. would make some final remarks about the person's character qualities that made them special and revisit something about the person that made everyone laugh.

Then he would say, "I would like to close now. And I just want to share four words with you: Everyone lives forever somewhere. And it's either heaven or hell." And then he would present the gospel.

He remembers this one guy in a wheelchair whose wife had died. And he did not want a funeral, but his kids said they had to do something. When J.P. gave the altar call, the guy went forward. J.P. just went down, knelt beside him, laid hands on him, and asked him to receive Christ—and he did!

Chapter 18
A Wedding Made Complete

One Saturday J.P. finished a wedding ceremony at the Dana Point Resort, and as he walked toward his car carrying a Bible, a limousine pulled up, the window rolled down, and a woman asked, "Are you a pastor?"

"Yes," J.P. replied.

The woman appeared frantic. "My daughter is supposed to get married, and the judge doing the wedding is late. Can you do it?" she asked breathlessly.

"I'm sure he's just caught in heavy traffic."

"He's already almost an hour late. Can you please help us?

"Okay," J.P. said, somewhat reluctantly.

When J.P. arrived at the venue, he discovered what the attendees had been doing for the hour-long wait. They had been drinking, and some were sloshed. He saw one young woman say to the groom, "Hey, it's not too late," and she lifted her skirt up in a suggestive way. It was obvious they weren't Christians.

Oh, my goodness, what am I going to do? J.P. thought as he watched the processional walk up toward the altar. He opened his remarks by talking about the benefits of a Christian marriage, and then he presented the gospel before they said their vows. After a brief prayer, he pronounced the couple husband and wife.

J.P. was a little angry at the spirit of the gathering. The whole thing was very, very short. And then he got out of there. He didn't want to talk to anybody, and he didn't get paid for it because he went away so fast.

Two months later that same couple J.P. married on the spur of the moment came to visit Ocean Hills Church in San Juan Capistrano. On their honeymoon, they watched the video of the wedding. God planted in their hearts a desire to know Him. Somehow, they tracked J.P. down, came to church, and received the Lord. They started going to church regularly.

Chapter 19

Launching Kathy's House Ministry

On June 12, 1994, the nation was shocked by the murder of Nicole Brown Simpson and the subsequent eleven-month trial of her ex-husband, the legendary football star O.J. Simpson.

During the "Trial of the Century," the public learned about a pattern of domestic abuse during their marriage that continued after their volatile separation. They reconciled, but the pattern of abuse continued. Audio released during the murder trial revealed desperate calls Brown made to 911 in October 1993, fearing for her life.

The lurid trial raised the public's awareness of domestic abuse, which led to God touching a few people's hearts about the urgent need to create shelters for women fleeing physical, verbal, emotional, or sexual abuse. Women in crisis, sometimes pregnant, often homeless, exerted a cry that could not be ignored.

Because of my turbulent past, I absorbed the societal awakening with a mounting sense that I must respond. I turned to our administrator, Roger Gales, working at the thrift store, and said, "We have to have a home for women and children!"

"I think you should do something ... you could start by raising some money," Roger replied.

The thrift store's location allowed us to meet many people in need. Sometimes women would come into the store who couldn't pay for their rent, utilities, or even food. If it didn't involve money, we could help them. Because J.P. was running the program, I didn't have a lot of say in it.

I was gripped by the need to help women in crisis but unsure how to start. J.P. was focused on helping troubled men, especially addicts, and did not feel called to get involved in women's issues. So, I began to research domestic abuse shelters available in Orange County.

I found one that started in 1979 in Anaheim called The Sheepfold. It had been launched by Fran Lundquist after a painful divorce and the suicide of her eighteen-year-old son. As Lundquist grieved over her circumstances one day, her face pressed into the tear-stained pages of a Bible, God gave her a vision for the shelter she ultimately launched, located about thirty-five miles away from our thrift store.

Closer to home was Laura's House, which opened in 1994, named after a victim of domestic abuse. But it was not faith-based. There was no one locally who had a faith-based shelter. I sent out sixty letters to people who would be willing to donate, and I had a huge response.

Remarkably, enough money came in from sixty letters to buy Kathy's House in 1995, the first Christ-centered shelter of its kind for women in South Orange County.

I called Fran Lundquist for advice, and she gave me her entire manual. Lundquist also told me not to put single women and women with children in the same home. "It doesn't work," she advised.

After I hung up the phone, I thought, *What if I buy a duplex? I can put single women on one side and women with children on the other.*

That's exactly what I decided to do. I couldn't say no to a single woman just because she didn't have a child. I wanted to help both. The duplex we bought was a little run down, but I had many volunteer men who would come in and do carpentry work or paint.

The thrift store supported the homes for the men and the women. We had a deal with our residents. Residents were expected to work in the store, and if they worked a year and graduated, we would provide them with a car upon graduation and pay for their first and last months' rent somewhere. We were not paying them anything. They were volunteers, not employees. That was what made the model so successful and allowed us to do things for them. We had free labor and free merchandise to operate the thrift store. All of the income went toward running the shelter homes.

We kept our office on the second floor of the thrift store. The word on the street said, "If you go upstairs to the second floor, you can get help." We would give them food.

> "Truly I tell you, whatever you did for one of the least of these brothers and sisters of mine, you did for me." (Matthew 25:40 NIV)

During the one-year program, we served the residents in the spirit of the Matthew 25. If they had to go to court, we took them to court. If there was a judgment or fine, and they didn't have any money, we helped them pay their debt. We took them to DUI classes; we helped them get a driver's license. We were with them for a long time, and it took a long time to help change their lives.

Chapter 20

Lori's Story

One of the early arrivals at Kathy's House was a woman named Lori, who came with her daughter Miranda. Lori came from a broken family and had become addicted to drugs and alcohol by the time she was twelve.

Lori told us her story. "My aunt was the first person who got me high," she told us. "I started at ten years old with marijuana, then the drinking, then the drug addiction."

She lacked a family support system because her mom and dad divorced when she was seven. Her dad was addicted to cocaine and other things, and her mom was codependent.

Lori's single mother found herself raising four children. By the time Lori's parents were sixteen and seventeen, they had started families and had four babies. So, they were babies raising babies. It was just toxic when Lori was growing up, and she got addicted to methamphetamine.

Lori continued her story. "In my heart, I wanted to change, but I just didn't know how. And I didn't have the right resources. Things got super bad after I got pregnant and had my daughter. I wasn't married. It was just basically me raising her. I didn't do any drugs when I was pregnant, but not long after she was born, I started back up."

A friend helped Lori move from Lakewood, California, to El Segundo, a relative island of calm surrounded by LAX, the ocean, and the Hyperion sewage treatment plant. "I got a job and got on my feet, but the problem was I still had the addiction, and I became the worst kind of addict."

The friend who invited her to El Segundo was in rehab and tried to help her, but her half-hearted attempts proved fruitless. "I became an isolated addict; I didn't want anyone to know. The drug addiction got super bad because the drugs weren't working anymore for me. I would just lie in bed and cry because the drugs weren't working."

In desperation, she cried out to God. "I would just beg God to help me, to please show me how to live because I didn't know how. I called every single church in that little town, trying to get someone to hear my heart. I remember talking to a couple of people, and they never called me back. And I just sank into this deep despair."

She continued to pray that God would send help.

At that time, Lori's daughter attended a preschool run by a local church. "I never talked to them. I didn't want anyone at the school to know what our life was like. It was my little secret." (Her daughter told the school staff her mommy was sad and cried a lot.)

She was surprised when something unexpected arrived in the mail. She opened a small card and read it: "Hi, Lori. My name is John. I'm the new minister at the church where your daughter goes to school, and I've heard nice things about you. I just thought we would invite you to church sometime."

Lori began to weep as she re-read the card. "Oh my God, is this is my e-ticket? I wondered."

She went to meet with Pastor John. "I was very worldly, and I went into his office in a super short miniskirt. I sat there telling him about my life, telling him I'm not an addict, I'm a victim of my circumstances. I believed that."

"He was a wonderful man, and God was so good about this whole thing."

One week later, Lori went to the welfare office in Inglewood with her daughter. "They check your bags for guns and stuff. I was just so scatterbrained about the drugs I didn't think they were going to check. And they opened my bag and found the drugs."

Lori's five-year-old daughter began to scream: "Don't take my mommy to jail! Don't take my mommy to jail!"

A welfare officer turned to Lori and said, "You need to call someone to get your daughter because you're probably going to be gone ninety days."

"Why is this happening now? I thought. My life is over, and I don't know who to call, because I don't want to talk to my family ... I'll call the minister."

Pastor John and his wife came to pick up Lori's daughter, and the police drove her from Inglewood to downtown L.A. to formalize her arrest. "When I got in there, I just remember sitting there crying and thinking my life's over. I'm gonna lose my daughter, I thought."

A detective went into another room and examined the drugs in her possession.

Then something surprising happened. The detective came back, stuck his finger in Lori's face, and said, "You better never do this again to your daughter."

The authorities released Lori, and the police gave her a courtesy ride back to the front door of her house, forty-five minutes away, and wished her well in her "new life."

"This doesn't happen, right? This doesn't happen, I thought."

When Lori arrived home, she immediately called Pastor John. "What are you doing home?" he asked. "They told me you would be gone ninety days ..."

"I can't explain it, Pastor John," she said.

The pastor and his wife reunited mother and daughter, who discovered an amazing love from that local congregation. "The church family embraced me like nobody ever had," she said. "I started going to church, and my whole attitude started to change. It felt like I was on this pink cloud. I never felt so much love in my whole life. God started revealing himself through these people because there was nothing for them to gain. I didn't have anything to offer them. But they loved me. And the love they showed me because of their love for God was something I'd never experienced."

Swept up in the Lord's tender embrace, Lori was born again and baptized at the church.

Pastor John set up a job interview for her with a computer company. "In my life when I worked, I was a cocktail waitress or something. I didn't have skills."

When Lori went in for the interview, they handed her a large pamphlet with questions about computers. Her eyes began to well up with tears. "I didn't want them to know I was crying, so I said, 'Do you think I have something in my eye?'

"They gave me the key for the bathroom down the hall, and I was in there for about forty-five minutes crying. I looked in the mirror and said, 'You know what? You're a drug addict, and that's all you'll ever be.' And so I left that interview. I went home, then I went and got drugs. I started hiding from my church family and was giving up."

Lori always wore dark glasses when she went to pick up her daughter at school. One day Pastor John saw her and asked, "How are you doing today, Lori? We miss you at church. We love you."

She didn't respond, but after she got home, she called the minister. "Look, Pastor John, I'm using again ... I don't deserve to have friends like you."

"Lori, God loves you no matter what. It doesn't matter how many times you fall; it matters how many times you pick yourself back up." His words resonated with her heart.

A week later was picture day at school. "I was high. I had stayed up all night. I was brushing my daughter's hair. She had to look perfect because nobody could know what was going on in my life. Her hair just would not cooperate. And next thing you know, it was past the time for her pictures.

"I felt like the biggest failure and the worst mother. I kicked her out of the bathroom. I shut the bathroom door, got a razor, and climbed in the bathtub.

"Today's a good day to die, I thought. I never felt deep despair like that before. I was close to ending my life, like no feeling was inside of me."

When Lori lowered herself into the tub to take her life, the still small voice of the Lord spoke to her heart: *Call the minister—911 ... Call the minister— 911.*

She called Pastor John, and within ten minutes, Lori's house was full of people from the church. The next day, she was at a treatment center in San Juan Capistrano.

Lori spent forty-two days in rehab while the pastor and his family took care of her daughter. "After that, I did another program, but you have to understand, I'm an addict and a manipulator. And I didn't like some of the rules and stuff, so they kicked me out because I had a bad attitude. I couldn't do it on my own. When I couldn't get myself out of bed to function, my daughter took care of me. And I felt like we needed to heal together."

At the second treatment center, she met someone who knew about Kathy's House.

"I just knew in my heart that was where God wanted me to take my daughter. After I got kicked out of that place, I waited a couple of weeks, and I got in touch with Kathy's House. I'll never forget the first day when they dropped us off in front of the thrift store.

"Then they took us to the house. We were the first residents on the mother and children's side. And it was amazing. I just really felt it was a good place to heal. And we had so much support. The tools they gave us were amazing. The first couple of weeks were great because they drove me everywhere. They were so loving and did everything for me."

But then God started to test Lori because she needed to become independent and develop personal responsibility. "After two weeks they gave me a bus pass, and I had a bad attitude about it.

"You don't know who I am, I thought. I'm not taking a bus. I just remember being so mad at God when I was on that bus."

One day Lori had three buses to catch, and she missed the second one. "I was just so mad at God. I told Him, 'I can't believe You're doing this to me.'"

Then the still small voice of the Lord spoke to her again: *Lori, I didn't do this to you. But I love you so much, I'm going through this with you.*

"That's when I started to surrender things to God."

During Lori's eight-month stay at Kathy's House, she went to court to settle legal matters from her past. On the last day Lori went to court, the judge took his gavel, slammed it down, and said, "Case dismissed. Now go, young lady, and sin no more."

Lori marveled at the Lord's providential care in her life. "It was God's hand in that whole thing because I truly thought I was a victim, not an addict, a victim of my circumstances. But at some point, I needed to accept responsibility for my actions and my choices, and I felt that was God's way of getting my attention and getting me to trust Him completely.

"Kathy's House was great because they gave us structure, they gave us tools. We were always busy doing activities. They wouldn't let us just lie around the house and do nothing. We had a routine. We always had daily Bible studies and went to church, and we would go to AA meetings." Lori's daughter began meeting with a Christian counselor.

Lori felt the Lord's presence while she stayed there. "At Kathy's House, I felt God all around me. My life is truly blessed beyond belief. You know, I've had the same job since I left there. He's given me a new life. It's better than I ever had before."

When it came time for Lori and her daughter to depart Kathy's House, her daughter did not want to leave. "She clung to the furniture with both her arms and legs. She didn't want to go. Oh my, it was so heartbreaking. She didn't want to leave her family there. We were family. We were sisters—all the women there felt the same. I'm still friends with all the girls from Kathy's House."

Lori went into the corporate world for two years, then we offered her the opportunity to work with us as a house supervisor at Kathy's House for two years. "I wanted to help the women with everything that was in me; I wanted to give back.

"You know what I have? I'm so blessed. I don't regret anything I've gone through because, today, it's made me who I am, and I have a lot of empathy for people who are suffering."

Chapter 21

Terry Martin's Passing

Terry Martin was a legendary surfboard shaper in Southern California. He shaped his first ten-foot board when he was only fourteen, using some balsa wood he found in a scrap pile. His first board was lighter, sleeker, faster, and more maneuverable than the typical "logs" out there, and there was considerable demand for his boards.

A gifted craftsman, Martin could shape wood or foam the way Michelangelo worked with marble. He went to work for Hobie Alter in 1963 and ultimately shaped more than 80,000 surfboards over his lifetime, although the exact number is unknown because Martin said he stopped counting after 50,000. He shaped boards for a long list of surfing luminaries, including Phil Edwards, Corky Carroll, Gerry Lopez, Rabbit Bartholomew, Gary Propper, and Joyce Hoffman.

We became friends with Terry Martin and his wife, Candy, because both of us couples shared a common faith and attended the same church.

At seventy-four, Terry got the unwelcome news he had developed an advanced case of melanoma. He had put off going to the doctor, and things progressively got worse and worse. When Terry was dying, J.P. would go and visit him every day. He had a hospital bed in his living room, and he would hold court. You could walk in and talk to him.

When he was getting close to the gate and hospice was coming in, he would say, "J.P., tell them that story about Carol." So, every surfer that came in heard that story.

The story about Carol he was referring to was the one we told in chapter five, describing the final moments before J.P. lost her due to diabetes complications. Just before she died, she told J.P., "I'm on a train, and it's very bright."

In Terry's final days, with his condition getting weaker and weaker, he turned to J.P. and said, "It's not bright, and I don't hear a train."

"You better get right, Terry," J.P. said, gently ribbing his friend.

He didn't take care of the melanoma, and it grew to this huge thing. He had a tumor the size of a baseball coming out of the side of his head. His whole stomach looked like a lizard.

One day when J.P. was visiting, Terry pulled up his shirt and said, "Doesn't that look like a volcano? See that red thing over there, like a boil. It hurts, but it's going to pop."

J.P. grimaced as he watched the boil start oozing. Terry was very inquisitive about what was happening to his body. He had his wits about him to the end.

A nurse who came over every day said she thought the doctors were gouging the insurance company because there was nothing else that could be done short of a miracle. He had been on all kinds of stuff, some natural, and they had to drain his lungs every two days. It was very painful.

In the end, the nurse informed Terry they would need to intubate him and make him comfortable. "What do you want for your last meal before we do that?" she asked.

"Tell Candy I want bacon and eggs and key lime pie."

J.P. marveled at the courage displayed by Terry Martin as he approached death. Terry died so well because of his faith in Jesus Christ, knowing something better awaited him on the other side.

Terry's ashes were under our bed for three years. Candy couldn't handle having his ashes. Terry's friends were going to do a paddle-out ten days later but never did it. He was under the bed in a box, and J.P. would talk to him.

Instead of the paddle-out, Terry's friends organized one of the largest memorial events ever seen in the surf industry. They held the event at the Ocean Institute in Dana Point, with an auction raising money to help support Candy. Like many shapers in the industry, Terry did not have a pension fund or other retirement savings available for her or a life insurance policy. "He had no money. Nobody who builds surfboards does it for the money. There's no money it," Royce Cansler, one of the event organizers, explained.

At least thirty surfboards, surf art, and many accessory items found their way into the event. Royce said, "We even auctioned off Terry's old Ford van that he used to drive to the factory. We decked it out, made sure it was running as good as it could, put one of Terry's old T-shirts on the seat, put a foam blank in the back, like he was off to the factory, and put some of his tools in. I think we got five or six thousand for it. It was an incredible auction."

Chapter 22

Jonathan's Story

I knew Jonathan from the day he was born. His father was a very close friend of mine. When Jonathan was eight to ten years old, he held the world's record for killing the biggest boar with a bow and arrow. His dad, an avid hunter, taught Jonathan how to use it. They would go all over the world game hunting. Jonathan had so much charisma, but he got into drugs at an early age. One point in time his parents didn't know where he was for a year. He was out of control.

Jonathan recalled being raised in a Christian home. "My parents went to Believer's Chapel in San Clemente with J.P and Carol, so I was raised in church," Jonathan said. "But I was a bit of a knucklehead from a very early age. I was very mischievous and got into a lot of trouble."

Remarkably, he sensed there was a spiritual battle for his soul as early as five years old. "I remember having a magnified view of the devil in my life and a very diminished view of God. I always thought the devil had so much power over me, and every time I cried out to God, I heard nothing. My prayer was always 'Change me, make me a better boy so I'm not always upsetting my parents.' I had a war going on inside myself. So, by about nine years old I made a conscious decision to walk away from the Lord completely."

Even as a preteen, Jonathan thought the gap between a holy God and his sinful behavior was insurmountable. "I loved the Lord and always believed in Jesus. My impression of God was, He's too good for this junk. I don't want to present my body as an offering to Him. Since I can't get it right, I'm just gonna walk away and take my medicine because if there's a God out there, He's holy and He wants nothing to do with me because

I'm junk. I made that vow to myself to not concern myself with trying to be good anymore."

In Jonathan's neighborhood in San Juan Capistrano, there were twenty-one kids, ranging in ages from ten to eighteen. "It was during the '80s, the punk rock era, and it was just mayhem," Jonathan recalled. "The older kids would drive us around and buy liquor. The older brothers would buy their younger brothers hard liquor, so liquor and marijuana were a constant at a very, very young age.

"I continued on that path and tried to put high school together but failed miserably. When I turned eighteen, I started getting locked up for drugs and other things."

Jonathan spent most of the 1990s in prison, from the time he turned eighteen until age twenty-six. To survive as a relatively young man in prison, he joined a white supremacist gang. "When I got there, I was terrified. It's all these older men, who were crazy, and I was a knucklehead. Out of fear, I did the thing that made the most sense to me, which was joining a gang to have their protection and be part of a family," he explained.

Three months into his first prison term, Jonathan's father passed away. J.P. remembers that excruciating moment. Jonathan's father was overweight, went running, and overdid it. He dropped dead of a heart attack at thirty-nine. Jonathan had to go to the funeral in handcuffs. It was a big embarrassment for him, but he wanted to be there.

Whenever Jonathan was paroled, it was usually short-lived. "I would get out of prison with hopes and dreams of doing well, and I would be back in within a week, maybe two weeks tops. I had no money and had to start all over. During this whole long season, I was not talking to my parents. When my dad passed away, our relationship was very rocky at the time, so that was hard."

Drugs were omnipresent in Jonathan's prison experience. He observed criminal activity, extortion, and violence, and got entrenched in the white supremacist lifestyle. "For the most part, the divisions are very racial," he noted.

On Thanksgiving Day 1999, Jonathan was paroled. He was determined to never return. "I felt like I was done with drugs and done with the prison lifestyle."

After his release he contacted his high school sweetheart. "She kicked me to the curb years ago because I was dumb and getting in trouble. And she said, 'You know, I've been waiting for you all these years. Are you ready?'"

They were married within three months of Jonathan's parole. A year later, they had a daughter.

"We always loved each other, and she knew me before I got into big trouble. We had a good relationship before that, but we were both still really dumb. We were both still drinking; I wasn't doing any drugs or crime. But suddenly, we had this new baby."

When Jonathan held his daughter in his arms for the first time in the hospital, he knew she was a gift from God and he would have to make significant changes in his life. He looked at her precious, tiny face and said, "I promise, you will never see your dad in prison."

He recognized the enormity of this gracious gift, but not the gift-giver. "I still wasn't walking with the Lord and had no relationship with Him. We started having problems in our marriage after our third child. This whole time I had been sober just on my willpower because I didn't want to go back to prison. But I was still in communication with all the gang members because I had friendships with them. The thing is, you don't get out of those things. They'll let you do good, but as soon as you step back into that lifestyle, you're back in full force, so then my marriage started falling apart.

"Some stuff happened in the bad marriage. From a lack of knowledge about what to do and not having a personal relationship with God, I turned back to my old ways. My wife took off. She split with another guy. So, I was raising my kids. I didn't get it for about the first nine months."

Jonathan had his hands full fathering three young children. At the same time, he had come down with hepatitis and was giving himself shots with interferon to try and get rid of it. "I was in a bad place. I was hurting for my marriage, and I was injecting myself with these things."

Interferon therapy is used to treat multiple sclerosis, some cancers, and hepatitis B and C. When used to treat hepatitis, patients often see reductions in liver damage and cirrhosis.

In Jonathan's case, however, he believes there was an unwelcome side effect from the therapy. "Interferon triggered a lot of psychological issues and cravings that came back. I was by myself, raising these kids, and it just was too much for me. I ended up relapsing."

"Things got really bad, and my kids went to live at my mom's house. I was just running on empty and strung out."

On Christmas Eve 2007, Jonathan found himself at a witch's house. "I was hanging out with some dark people, and she was one of my friends. She offered to read my tarot cards. I was messed up, and we were doing drugs together."

The witch asked if she could read Jonathan's future using tarot cards.

"Yeah, whatever," Jonathan replied.

She began to read each card after she flipped it over.

Suddenly, a still small voice spoke to Jonathan's heart with a blunt warning: *If she turns over the next card, you will die right here in your seat.*

The witch began to turn the next tarot card over, but

Jonathan's arm lunged forward and slapped the card out of her hand before it could be turned over.

He jumped to his feet, knowing he must leave immediately. "When I got up, there was a manifestation of a full-blown demon standing between me and the doorway. It was the most horrific thing I had ever seen, with a body that looked like a big, charred piece of charcoal, with a mutilated, melted face, and a goat horn in the middle of his forehead. It was about eleven feet tall and smelled like hell, like sulfur, eggs, and rotted carcass."

He looked back to see if the witch was seeing what he was. She looked at Jonathan and let out a fiendish, diabolical laugh.

Jonathan put his shoulder down as if he was about to go through an imposing football lineman, reached through the demon to grab the doorknob, opened it, and fled down the stairs, with the smell of hell lingering on his clothing. "I couldn't get the smell off after walking through that thing. I drove straight to my mom's house and went to her garage. I hadn't talked to my mom in months."

Jonathan's family gathered at his mother's house to celebrate Christmas the next morning. "My kids were there, but I didn't interrupt them. This was a bad moment, and I was in bad shape. So I just opened the garage door and went in the garage, I got one of the sleeping bags out of the attic, lay down in the garage, and went to sleep."

No one knew Jonathan was sleeping in the garage until he emerged the next morning like a mummy returning from the dead. They greeted him with saccharine smiles and expressions of "Merry Christmas," but he knew immediately he had disrupted their peaceful gathering. "I could see the pain I had caused everyone on their faces, from my kids, to my mom, to every family member."

He went into the kitchen and began to ruminate. "They were all trying to have a good Christmas, and I felt like I ruined it just by being there.

"I felt the enemy on me, and I grabbed a sushi knife, snuck out the back, got in my van, and drove down to the landfill. I was going to kill myself. I had a Sharpie marker in the car, and I wrote the word 'peace' on the dashboard of the van. I walked up the two miles to the landfill. I wanted everyone to have peace and thought if I ended my life, the nightmare I brought upon myself and others would be over.

"After walking two miles, I ducked behind a bush and retrieved the knife from my pocket. I don't remember thinking about praying. I don't remember thinking about God. I don't remember anything. I just wanted it to be over.

"I immediately swung the knife as hard as I could at my wrist. But something grabbed my arm in midair and would not let me do it. I was fighting with this thing. Unseen, totally invisible. I thought I was having a mental breakdown, fighting with this thing."

Suddenly the presence of God fell on Jonathan. He felt a warm sensation, and the landscape appeared wavy. "God took me in the Spirit through my whole life, all these places where bad stuff happened to me, where hurts happened. He showed me the resentment and unforgiveness I had been carrying were killing me, consuming me. He showed me He was there with me the entire time, and He never left."

Then the Lord impressed on his heart: *This unforgiveness is killing you. You have an opportunity to give it to Me. Do you trust Me with it? If you trust Me to make it all right, I will set you free right now, and I will walk with you every day for the rest of your life.*

Jonathan broke down and started weeping. "Take it, take it, take it ..." he sobbed.

"Then I felt like a waterfall coming out of heaven. It showered me, and I felt the darkness leave my body, in every way, shape, and form. It felt like I was being delivered from a legion of demons. I was washed and clean!"

The last words imparted to Jonathan's heart were these: *Go back where you came from.*

When Jonathan stood up, he felt like his spine had been strengthened, as if it had been refashioned with titanium. "My gaze went from looking at the ground to looking straight ahead down the path. I had been holding my head down in shame for so long."

He walked back to his van, not knowing how much time had passed. "People were still at my mom's when I got back there. I walked in the door completely sober, completely in my right mind, supernaturally delivered and healed."

After he walked through the front door, his mother rushed over to him and said, "I'm so glad you came back!" She immediately noticed a dramatic change in his countenance, as did others at the family gathering.

Later, Jonathan reflected on the dramatic events that changed the course of his life. "I encountered God for myself, and I knew He loved me. I knew He covered my sins. I knew He made me a promise He was going to be with me for the rest of my life, no matter what.

"It took a lot to get my attention."

...

For the next three years, Jonathan parked his van at The Vineyard Church in Laguna Niguel and attended their ministry school. "I was so hungry for God, everything in my life had to be about Him," he said.

After that, he spent over a year at the International House of Prayer in Kansas City to work on inner healing. "I was still in love with my ex-wife, and I knew I had to get that stuff out of me," he remembered. "She was with many other men by then, and thinking about it was a trigger. So, that was the only time I stepped away from my kids, which was the hardest thing ever."

After Jonathan moved back to California, he began working at a homeless center known as I Hope. "One day I relapsed, and I hadn't in a long time. It's the most horrific thing ever. I had mental health issues because of all the drugs in my background, so I had severe psychosis and schizophrenia. And I'd have episodes every couple of months—severe ones—that I now view as spiritual attacks.

"I went through a few of those relapses as a Christian, and they're horrible," he said. He was ready to give up on his faith when God arranged a divine appointment with J.P.

After listening to Jonathan's story, J.P. offered his wisdom: "You have all these good things going on in your life," he said. "You've got a loving family, you've got a good job, you're surrounded by Christians. You messed up, but get up and dust yourself off."

Jonathan began dating a strong Christian named Sharise, who happened to have a roommate studying to become an ultrasound technician. "She wanted to practice on some people doing ultrasounds so she could pass her test. I had been really tired lately, which I thought was from doing all the drugs. So I said, 'Hey, you can practice on me.'

"I got this scan, and during it, she turned white as a ghost."

Jonathan looked at her and said, "What's going on? Do you see something that shouldn't be there?"

"It looks like you have a pretty large tumor on your kidney ... about the size of a baseball ... and it's attached to your adrenaline gland."

"It's under my ribcage, right?" he asked.

She told him it was close to being able to metastasize—one bump and it could have gone everywhere. "You need to go to the hospital right away, and you need to tell them exactly what I just told you."

Despite the jolting revelation, Jonathan says the peace of God fell on him in that moment.

Doctors later confirmed he had a very aggressive renal cell sarcoma—kidney cancer. They said it would be resistant to chemotherapy and radiation. The only prospect they offered was surgery to remove as much as possible and then hope for the best. It was unlikely, they said, he would ever be in remission.

Jonathan did not have medical insurance or the means to pay for surgical intervention. "J.P. was walking this out with me. I had just started this mailbox store but had very little money coming in. I couldn't qualify for MediCal because of the business. They're telling me I need surgery right away."

Jonathan learned it would cost $7000 for the operation, not including additional costs due to the hospital and anesthesiologist.

The Lord moved on J.P.'s heart, and he went to meet directly with the surgeon, probing to see if the man would lower his fee. At first, the surgeon was adamant, telling J.P. he would not lower the price.

"Jonathan wants you to do the surgery," J.P. told him. "He has confidence in you, and, you know, trust is everything to a patient."

"I'm not going to do it!" the surgeon replied.

J.P. continued to barter, trying to find some compromise.

Finally, the surgeon relented. "Okay, I'll tell you what I'll do. I have two women in the office and all they do is deal with insurance companies and the government. It would take me a year to get reimbursed, and at the end of the day, I'll net $1500. I'll do it for $1500."

J.P. quickly agreed, joking later it would cost more than that to get his transmission rebuilt.

"I got the best surgeon," Jonathan said. "He was the best guy that could have done this."

The outcome of the surgery was a great success. "I knew I would never have cancer again. The peace of God was unbelievable. I did not waver one single bit, and I've been cancer-free ever since."

Jonathan has one kidney, but doctors have told him the single kidney operates as capably and efficiently as if he had two.

...

Five years later, Jonathan developed what doctors initially thought was a kidney stone. It was a blood clot that choked the blood flow to his one remaining kidney.

"They sent me home to try and pass the kidney stone. But meanwhile, my kidney was dying because it was getting no blood. I had a fever and got really bad.

"When I went back in, they discovered my kidney was pretty much at ten percent. I was so sick, I didn't even know how to pray. I couldn't keep any food down. I didn't eat for forty days, not one single thing. I could not keep fluid down. They started dialysis right away. I was in the hospital forever. Every time I would get out of the hospital, I would have to be back within two hours. My blood pressure was so high I was on the verge of a stroke. I was dying."

J.P. tried to encourage Jonathan to remain positive, but the crisis summoned painful memories of J.P.'s first wife, Carol, who died while on kidney dialysis.

Even worse, doctors discovered Jonathan was among a very rare group of people allergic to the filtration system on the dialysis machine. "Every time, instead of feeling better after dialysis, I would get sicker."

Jonathan was finally able to make it home, and J.P. came to visit him and sat on the couch next to him. Jonathan poured out his heart. "J.P., I don't know if I'm gonna die. I can't even pray. I can't even believe … I don't know how to get out of this. Cancer was nothing compared to this. My kids hear me through the walls throwing up, day and night. I don't want them to worry, but they can see how skinny I am."

J.P. was moved with compassion for his friend. "Sometimes you don't know how to pray," he told him. "That's why we're here because we're gonna believe, and we're gonna pray for you, and we're gonna believe for you. You don't have to have the strength. This is where we come in."

Because of his illness, Jonathan had not been to church in a long time. But suddenly, he felt compelled to go. He drove to Heritage Church in San Clemente. "I was sitting in the back, and one of the guys sitting next to me, when we were walking out said, 'Dude, you really gotta go get some prayer.'"

After being on dialysis four days a week, Jonathan didn't feel like getting prayer. "I had been prayed for so many times. I thought this was my lot. I just accepted it, but I turned around and walked to the front anyway."

As he approached several women praying at the front of the church, Jonathan broke down in tears. "They just surrounded me and started praying. And I couldn't tell you what was prayed. I didn't feel anything. I didn't feel any better. But I walked out, and I thought it was the right thing to do, to get as much prayer as I possibly could."

Two days later, Jonathan went back for dialysis treatment. "At the end of my treatment, they tested my levels."

Then something remarkable happened that surprised the doctors.

"Your numbers have been deteriorating this whole time, but suddenly, they're getting rapidly better!" one of the doctors exclaimed.

"What?" Jonathan said.

Another nurse and doctor entered the room and were standing around Jonathan, staring at him in disbelief. "What's going on?" one asked.

"I don't know what's going on. You guys are the doctors ..."

"Your numbers are getting so much better we will have to change something when you come back in two days if this keeps happening."

Two days later doctors gave Jonathan the stunning news they wouldn't continue dialysis. "Your kidney made such an improvement, it will do more harm than good if we do that," they said.

Today, Jonathan is a walking miracle. An x-ray of his kidney revealed that three-fourths of it is dead. "I've got twenty percent of one kidney functioning, and it works as if both kidneys are fully functioning.

"The doctor says I've got a super kidney!"

Chapter 23

Feeding Sudan

In late 2013, the South Sudanese Civil War broke out between government and opposition forces, with Ugandan troops fighting alongside the South Sudanese government.

About 400,000 people are believed to have been killed in the war. More than 1.8 million people were internally displaced, with the rest fleeing to neighboring countries. Fighting in the agricultural areas of the south caused the number of people facing starvation to skyrocket to 6 million, causing famine in many areas, according to BBC News.

One of the scandals of the war was shadowy arms dealers selling weapons to both sides. In 2014, a Chinese arms manufacturer delivered 95,000 assault rifles and 20 million rounds of ammunition to the government, "providing enough bullets to kill every person in South Sudan twice over," Peter Martell reported in *First Raise a Flag: How South Sudan Won the Longest War but Lost the Peace*, his book detailing the history of the conflict.[1] Not to be outdone, one American arms dealer sold the government three Russian-made Mi-24 attack helicopters and two fighter jets, delivered by Hungarian mercenaries.

"The arms-buying spree took place against the economic collapse of South Sudan. By the end of 2014, South Sudan achieved the dubious honor of being ranked the number one failed state in the entire world," Martell wrote.[2]

More than 65 percent of the South Sudanese population (4.9 million people) needed food urgently, according to the World Food Programme, with at least 100,000 in imminent danger of death due to starvation.

Making matters worse, areas of South Sudan did not have rain for two years. "Our worst fears have been realized," declared Serge Tissot, with the U.N. "Many families have exhausted every means they have to survive."[3] He described how war has disrupted their agricultural life as farmers. "They've lost their livestock, even their farming tools. For months there has been a total reliance on whatever plants they can find and fish they can catch."[4]

Amidst this backdrop, Pastor Roger Gales at Heritage Church talked about the food emergency in Sudan at a Sunday service in 2015.

We sat there listening, moved by the pastor's description of the crisis. That night I went to bed and had a dream about a little Sudanese boy with big brown eyes, wearing a filthy, striped T-shirt. He said, "Could you please help? Could you feed me?"

I woke up filled with compassion and began to brainstorm with J.P. about ways to help. "Are we ever retiring from serving God?" I asked J.P.

"No," he replied.

"So, why do I have a retirement account at Kathy's House? What good is that?"

After praying and seeking the Lord's wisdom, we ultimately decided to give away nearly half of my retirement account to feed one million children and adults in Sudan.

I had just read an article about a young Frenchman in his twenties who wanted to help the Sudanese people. He said it starts with one person. I thought, okay, that's it! We'll be the one person, and then others will join.

Rallying the support of the church, we had a weekend event when all the small groups at church came together, and over the next several days we put food packets together.

The retail price of a meal was about fifty cents, and we could get one million meals on a forty-foot container because they are all freeze-dried.

During the process, we met Denise Carlsen, a missionary serving in Northern Uganda near the Sudanese border. She had been going back and forth between Uganda and South Sudan, working with Sudanese refugees. We thought she was a great conduit once the food hit the ground as she could supervise the food when it was distributed through the churches.

Then J.P. went to Northern California.. He had a connection with YWAM, and they provided another million meals. So J.P. got another forty-foot container, but it cost $24,000 to send it and do all the paperwork and everything.

I was grateful God gave me the dream about the Sudanese boy. It only takes one person to start a movement. We felt this was our cause.

CRACKED VESSELS

Chapter 24

Jason's Story

Jason Welsh grew up in San Bernardino, California, the third of three sons. "My dad was never in the home, so that kind of led to certain actions," Jason recalls. "I got saved when I was twelve, but I didn't have any discipleship or mentorship."

He submitted to the local gang culture and the things of the world. "At twenty-two, I was living at home and taking care of my mom. And she fell sick because she did a lot of dope, like crack cocaine. She was deteriorating, had a couple of strokes, and kept going to the hospital because she had seizures."

A heated disagreement erupted among family members, with accusations flying that she was not receiving adequate care. "They weren't taking care of her; they didn't even talk to her. I was taking care of her, but doctors weren't giving her the right dosage of seizure medicine, so the family felt like I was not doing my job correctly."

When Jason's mother fell into a coma, a combative confrontation ensued, and Jason moved out. "I just walked away and went into the streets. I no longer had a place to live. I was homeless."

He lived under a freeway overpass near Loma Linda Hospital and often got fed with the help of a food bank operated by the Rock Church. "When I couldn't get food there, I would go to the am/pm and get food out of the trash can," he recalled. "I had people who would help me by putting my bag aside so that I could have clean food. But then I had others who didn't like me getting food; they would just throw it in the dumpster. And so, I would have to pick out the good pieces, stuff that didn't have any trash on it.

"I did that for a couple of years. I was committing crimes, breaking into garages that were open. I would steal tools and stuff because I was trying to get dope. I almost died two times trying to feed my addiction."

Amidst a series of unwise decisions, he made one colossal error in judgment. "I robbed a drug dealer, which was not a good idea. He had been searching for me for months, trying to kill me. And he finally caught up with me in the bottom of a house basement."

The dealer sat in a chair in the basement facing Jason, with his hand clutching a gun on his lap. The man smirked. "I've been waiting for this day."

Jason realized he was trapped. If he tried to run up the stairs to the only door leading out of the basement, he would easily be shot. "I just sat there and started thinking about my end."

Then something happened that surprised Jason. While Jason's fate was twisting in the wind, the man began to smoke dope, and his harsh countenance softened. Then the man barked, "Get out of here. I never want to see you again!"

Jason believes God spared his life by inexplicably softening the man's heart—one of several of Jason's brushes with death.

"I was burning people—taking advantage of people to get money. I did it again to some other gang members. One was from the Mexican Mafia, and he was going to kill me. The other one was a local Mexican gang member. So, they caught up with me, three of them."

They grabbed Jason and held his arms up, while one of the men stabbed Jason repeatedly in the torso with a shiny object that appeared to be a knife. Jason slumped to the ground, and the men ran off.

Curled up on the ground, Jason felt the places they stabbed him, expecting to find blood, but didn't find any. *This doesn't hurt ... I think they stabbed me*, Jason thought. "I saw the light shining off the silver blade. I was holding myself, but there was no blood."

He believes that somehow—perhaps by divine intervention—God spared his life once more.

A couple of months later, a guy found Jason in his tent. "I burned him for his cell phone. He acted like he was my friend and brought me to his house. After I walked in, he hit me from behind and knocked me through a window, which gashed my arm. I was gushing blood, but I didn't have healthcare because I'm homeless, so I just held it together.

"I finally went to a hotel after I made a little bit of money. The police caught me there because I had a stolen car to get around. The car keys were left in it, so I popped the window. I was driving all around, acting like the car was mine, and it wasn't mine."

Jason landed in jail and began to deal with an accumulation of past transgressions, violations he would now have to deal with in the court system. A friend named Charlie came to visit him and said, "I'm sorry to hear about everything that happened."

"Did you know all the stuff that happened to me?"

"No, I mean with your mom."

"What happened to my mom?" Jason asked.

"She's dead ... she died of an aneurysm. They were operating on her, and she died on the table."

Jason grieved heavily at the loss of his mother. "She raised me by herself because my dad was not in the picture. She wanted me to be a man of God. I failed her," he lamented.

Jason begged the court to allow him to go to his mother's funeral. The judge shook his head and told him, "You've got crimes in three different cities. I can't let you go because you're a flight risk."

He returned to his cell disconsolate and dejected. His mind swirled with painful memories. *I failed my mom. I failed my family. I failed my community. I'm going to prison just like my older brother and my dad. How can I be in the same position as my father, someone who was never in my life and whom I despise? How am I in this position?*

Jason decided he would commit suicide by using a bed sheet, tying it around his neck, and throwing himself off the second tier of his dorm room in the West Valley Jail in San Bernardino.

While Jason tied his sheet to the top tier and prepared to jump, the still small voice of the Lord spoke to him: *Now that everyone's gone, what do you want to do?*

"What do you mean, everyone's gone? What do I want to do? I'm doing what I want to do."

The Lord pressed him. *What do you want to do?*

I want to follow You, Jason replied, dropping the sheet to the floor and surrendering his life to Jesus Christ. He began to follow Jesus wholeheartedly after that moment.

Jason served twenty-eight months at Folsom State Prison, the second-oldest prison in California, opened in 1880. It holds the distinction of being the site of two live performances by Johnny Cash in 1968.

"I went to prison preaching the gospel," he said. "I was in the same cellblock—the D block—where Johnny Cash was. A point system determined Jason's placement at the prison. "I was only one point away from maximum security, reserved for the most vicious criminals, where you're locked down twenty-three hours a day. I was level three. I was still in there with killers, but I was preaching the gospel to them. Some had muscles bigger than my head. When I preached to them, they would start cussing or smoking, or get up and leave. I had the Nation of

Islam and others trying to recruit me because they saw the anointing on me. I didn't know Scripture yet, but I started reading the Bible. God told me to read the Bible, eat my food, and work out."

A high school dropout, Jason was able to earn his GED, an alternative to a high school diploma, while incarcerated.

"God just totally took care of me. An older Christian guy became a father to me and began to mentor me. I mean, it was just amazing. He sent people in there that were putting money on my books. After they got out, they would send money to my account."

As Jason prepared to leave prison, the Lord spoke to his heart again: *Jason, now that you're getting ready to go, are you going to do what everybody else does?*

"What is that, Lord?" Jason asked.

They find Me in here, but they also leave Me in here.

"Lord, I'm not going to leave without You," he declared.

After his parole, he went to live temporarily with his eighty-two-year-old grandmother, a woman who served the Lord faithfully throughout her life. Jason told her he had an encounter with Jesus in prison and intended to serve him.

The first night he was at her home, a cousin came by, and they went out to a club. "I ended up getting something to drink. I thought, *No, this is not good. Jesus just asked me what I was going to do ...*

Suddenly Jason remembered a Christian counselor in the prison had recommended Set Free Ministries to him after his release. A flash of heavenly inspiration gripped him, and he decided, "I'm going to Set Free!"

Set Free bused Jason to Cabazon. Their facility in Cabazon was affiliated with United Community Outreach, the organization J.P. founded.

"I had twenty-eight days of beans, rice, and Jesus Christ," Jason says. "Forty guys were sleeping on the floor of a single-wide mobile home. For lunch, they had onion soup, which was water with a little onion in it."

After twenty-eight days, a visitor showed up who would become a key figure in Jason's life. "I see an older gentleman who has got on glasses, and he's a very committed Christian guy. His humor made people laugh. I came to find out it was Joseph Paul Spitz—J.P."

"I have room for one more man at our ranch in Lake Elsinore," J.P. told them.

Jason's hand shot up in the air, knowing he would have to get permission from his parole officer because of the distance. "I wasn't supposed to go over fifty miles away, but I talked to my parole officer, and he said, 'You know what, don't worry.'

"While I was there, notable and recorded miracles happened. They were serving so many people. We saw so many things happen on that ranch, on the men's home they established, so they could get their lives back together and reconnect with their families. The goal was to get you from the home into society. After a year of working with them, they would help you transition to the next level of life.

"This is when I was called to ministry. J.P. stepped in like a spiritual father to help me, to guide me. He said, 'You know, you have an anointing on your life, and I want to help steward that. I want to be a blessing of that. And I want to give you some wisdom and tell you some of my mistakes, and I'm going to tell you some ways I've been able to be successful.

"That's kind of the role he's played in my life. When I met J.P. and Diana, they became my family. They treated me with love and respect, and they were a part of my healing process. They said, 'You're going to be a man of God.'"

The first month Jason arrived at the ranch, he began attending a church nearby with the other men. "It was the first month my future wife, Sonia, showed up at the same church. At that time, we couldn't talk to women. We both gave our testimony and hit it off, even though we didn't talk."

Later, Jason went to J.P. and asked if he could date Sonia, and J.P. was willing to make an exception after Jason told him he believed Sonia was the one he would marry.

After Jason and his fiancé began attending church together, one woman boldly approached Sonia with a word for the wise. "The lady told her you better be ready to be with this guy because he is going to be a pastor. And you need to let him know, if you're not prepared to walk that walk, let him go right now."

Sonia knew what she was getting from Jason. Both had their sights set on ministry and married a short time later. "J.P. and Diana were part of our wedding. If it wasn't for them, we would not have had the wedding we were supposed to have.

"J.P. and Diana have been an inspiration in our lives. They taught us how to manage our money and so much else. They taught us how to be a man and a woman. Through us, their legacy continues."

After Jason left his twelve-month program at the Ranch, he worked at a swimming pool construction company before he and Sonia planted Amazing Church, located in a shopping center in Lake Elsinore. The church quickly mushroomed from sixty people to about 250. Our ministry helped launch the church, supplying the first and last months' rent for Jason's lease.

"The church is growing; the church is packed," Jason reported. "We have to put chairs outside. We've had people come to our church that heard me preaching from Stater Brothers Market. I love open-air preaching," he said.

"I love serving, doing whatever I can, because I love Jesus."

Chapter 25

A Tragic Accident

In the summer of 2019, the Spitzes' five-year-old grandson Zachary was playing with friends along the Snake River near Homestead, Oregon.

They were at a beach area having a picnic, and Zachary was playing with his brother and his best friend near the water. Many of his classmates were there. His mom, Rachel, had her back turned away from him, so she didn't see what was happening. She was facing the other way.

Suddenly a jet ski came roaring toward the beach, out of control. The young rider didn't know how to operate it properly, and as it headed toward the beach, the rider jumped off immediately before it hit the land.

It went on the beach and was headed right at Zachary, and Zachary did his Ninja move. That's what he does. He loved the Ninjas and wanted to be one when he grew up.

Teenage Mutant Ninja Turtles was an animated series that followed four turtle brothers, Leonardo, Michelangelo, Donatello, and Raphael, who fought malevolent entities in New York City.

Zachary pushed his brother and his friend out of the way like he had seen Ninja Warriors do on TV and saved them both! Tragically, however, Zachary suffered a fatal injury.

The town responded with an outpouring of grief, as well as a sweet expression of love. The entire town lined up for a mile with signs that Zachary's family saw on the way home from the hospital.

Zachary had lingered for a short time, and doctors

attempted to relieve the pressure on his brain caused by the traumatic injury. The townspeople were there waiting for the family because they knew he was about to be taken off all the mechanical devices because he was just a vegetable.

During that time, we were able to buy a mobile home in San Juan Capistrano for homeless men, and we named it Zachary's House. His mother came to see the shelter. In the living room, we have Zachary's photo and the story about how he saved the lives of others.

She wept when she saw it. She just loved it ... it brought her so much comfort.

(We included this story because Zachary was our grandson and a warrior for the Lord. He stood in the way so his friends would be saved, and that meant so much to our family.)

Chapter 26

Eric's Story

When Eric Hall was three days old, he was adopted into the family of a Navy SEAL and his wife in Montclair, California. "My dad was my best friend, my mentor, everything to me. He taught me all the good traits I have," Eric said. He describes his mother as a good woman who was "in the background."

As a child, Eric attended a Baptist school and was baptized when he was six.

After Eric's father returned from the Korean War, he became a Hells Angel. Eric explained there are different kinds of Hells Angels. "My dad wasn't so much the outlaw type," he said. "Eighty percent of Hells Angels are vets and own companies."

His dad ran his construction firm, installing underground utilities. Eric began working with him at nine years old. "I was operating bulldozers when I was twelve. I grew up with that atmosphere, but at the same time, I mixed with the Hells Angels.

"I did everything my dad did. When kids were playing football on the street, I was at work with my dad. I went to school, but every chance I had, I was with my dad. I didn't run around with my friends too much."

His parents began attending the Mormon church, and Eric went with them sporadically during high school. He met a young woman in the church who became his wife. "I got my girlfriend pregnant, so at seventeen I was married, and we had twins."

Two years later, Eric received the devastating news that his father had bladder cancer and was not expected to live. "I'm a teenager, I'm married, and I'm running around on motorcycles with my dad and the fellas and stuff, and when I'm nineteen, my dad died."

Emotionally, Eric fell apart. "I pretty much died with him. I was mad at God and mad at the world. All my morals went out the window."

Eric had been "prospecting" for the Hells Angels when his father passed away. "I became the youngest Hells Angels ever to get a full patch. Now you have to be twenty-one, so I'll always be the youngest Hells Angel ever.

"I got super involved in the club, roaming the earth, devouring who I may," he recounted. "It was an ugly, ugly life. I was strung out on drugs, manufacturing methamphetamine by the hundreds of pounds." His club name was Maniac, which he tattooed prominently on his upper body.

One evening Eric and his wife went out to dinner but came home earlier than their babysitter expected. "My wife's little brother was watching our twin daughters. So I walked in the door and I couldn't find my daughters or him. I walked into the bathroom, and he was in the bathtub with my daughters, naked."

Eric lost his mind. "You have five minutes to get him out of here!" he yelled, his face turning a deep shade of crimson. Eric's wife hurriedly put the young man in the car and drove him back to her parents in Moreno Valley.

Eric waited twenty minutes and then drove to his in-laws. "I passed her on the freeway because she was coming back. I walked into her mom and dad's house."

Eric hugged his mother-in-law, shook her dad's hand, and said, "Do you guys know I love you?"

Then Eric took three steps back, pulled out a .45, and shot their son sitting in between them.

Airlifted by paramedics to Loma Linda Hospital, the

young man flatlined three times, but remarkably, survived the shooting.

Eric was tried for attempted murder, even though it came out in the trial that his brother-in-law molested Eric's twin daughters, then two and a half years old. During the proceedings, the charge was reduced to involuntary manslaughter and finally lowered to discharging a firearm within the city limits.

At the sentencing, the judge looked at Eric and said, "Mr. Hall, given all the circumstances, I get it. I would have probably done the same thing."

Sentenced to six years, he served eight because he got involved in two stabbings. "I learned new tricks, and things got worse when I got out," he recalled.

After his release, Eric and his team of twelve in the Hells Angels continued their malicious, malevolent mayhem. "I was shot in the face with a .38 at close range in a bar and lived through it. I've got stab wounds all over me. One missed my heart by a quarter of an inch. I mean, I've been run over, fallen off a hundred-mile-an-hour motorcycle, and on and on and on. And I'm still here."

One night four rival gang members from the Mongols came to Eric's home, armed with fully automatic weapons, intending to kill Eric and his family. His modest home was fortified with wrought-iron fencing around the perimeter, a Rottweiler in the backyard, wrought iron on the front door, and an alarm system.

When he saw the four men busting through the fencing, he put his wife and two daughters in the bathtub and grabbed the gun his father left him, a Ruger Super Blackhawk .44 magnum, which he kept on his nightstand.

"It's the kind of gun that Clint Eastwood used," he noted. "My dad was like a cowboy. Being the son of a Navy SEAL, I went shooting with him. He taught me how to fight; he taught me military tactics. I've never been in the military, but I have military training."

First, the intruders shot and killed Eric's dog in the yard. "They semi-knew what they were doing. They had one trying to come in the front door, one coming from the back, and two from the sides. They're trying to cover every door so you can't escape. That's a police tactic. If the police raid your house, they're going to cover every window. Every exit of that house they're going to have a gun pointed at it. If you're an outlaw, you study cops and how they do things.

"I killed all the lights in the house and set the alarm off. Now my alarm is going whoo whoo whoo. It's linked to the police, so the police are coming. I don't care if I go to jail. I don't care about anything but my wife and kids. I want the police here ASAP."

One at a time, each of the assailants began to kick a door in. Eric positioned himself next to his chimney, a few feet inside his sliding glass door. "I waited until every one of them came in the house because I couldn't shoot anybody outside the house."

As the first man came through the door, Eric pointed and fired. The first man went down. "I go around through the kitchen, and this guy is coming around to the side door because I can hear him rattling it."

When the second man came in, Eric shot him as well. "Through all this, my kids are screaming, and my wife is screaming. It stinks with the smell of gunpowder coming out, people are screaming, people are making noises. It's a mess."

Eric shot the final two gang members as they came through the doors. "A .44 kicks hard," he explained. "You can shoot a .44 through an engine block. If you get shot in the hand with a .44, it's gonna rip your arm off your body. You're not gonna survive. Very seldom are you gonna survive any type of wound from a .44 mag. So anyway, they all passed away."

The authorities had arrived when the fourth gang

member entered the house. "They set up a perimeter. There were helicopters in the air. When everything was done, I let the police in the house and I got arrested and went to jail. I was in county jail for three years fighting that."

Eventually, the four deaths were ruled justifiable homicides, and Eric was released. "The police department said if I didn't have a firearm, I would be dead and so would my family. So that was a big statement that helped me in court. I didn't shoot anybody in the back and didn't shoot anybody outside of my house. They were all in the house armed, with fully automatic weapons. I wasn't out of bounds in any of that, except for being an ex-felon with a firearm. I shouldn't have had a firearm. Thank God I did, or I would have been in trouble."

After Eric was released from custody, he returned to his evil ways. "My whole thing was just drugs and violence. That's all I knew ... you can imagine the life of a Hells Angel."

He paid a price for his felonious behavior, and ultimately received eight prison terms, spending a total of twenty-three years in prison. "There are thirty-three prisons in the state of California, and I've been to twenty-eight," he says. He was shipped from prison to prison because he was constantly getting in trouble.

In his final term, he instigated a riot. "I got shot, stabbed, tear-gassed, pepper sprayed, all that good stuff, and went to the hole, solitary confinement. You don't have a cellmate, they feed you through the slide, you get thirty minutes a day out of your cell, and other than that you're slammed in that cell. You don't leave it."

One night, sitting on his prison bunk, he began to weep uncontrollably, something unfamiliar for such a hard-hearted man. "You're talking about a very vicious, violent person. I don't do crying. I don't get scared. I don't do fear. It's not in me.

"I just felt super heavy and I started crying, pouring down tears. I felt I was slipping into insanity. I tried to wrap my mind around that. It came to a point where I felt like my next thought was gonna go into insanity."

At the same time, the fear of God gripped his heart. "I was scared, shaking, crying, pouring tears."

Eric dropped to his knees in the cell and cried out to a God he didn't know. "Lord, if You will deliver me from this, I'll serve You all the days of my life. Just continue to show me Your face every day. I give You my life."

With Eric's heart cry, he found redemption. "God showed up. I had a sense of peace I never had before. I've had millions of dollars, and I've been broke. I've been homeless. I've had power, and I've been nobody. But the thing I wanted my whole life and never had was peace. I didn't even know what peace looked like."

Eric became a new creature in Christ. "From that point forward, I was in the Bible the next day and stayed in the Word, stayed on my knees. The Lord shows up every time I call on Him. Everything I asked Him, He answered. It's not always what I want to hear, but I get an answer. I get convicted constantly. He is breaking chains in me constantly."

Eric met his second wife, Jody, through another inmate during his incarceration. "She came to see me while I was in prison," he said. Jody happened to manage the thrift store which supported Kathy's House. She asked Jonathan Phillips to write Eric a letter while he was still an inmate.

Eric got that first letter from Jonathan two days after he surrendered his life to God.

"I was still in the hole, and he started mentoring me. We're writing to each other. He asked me, 'What do you need? What can I do for you?' He prayed for me on the phone and began praying for me regularly."

After a short time, Eric applied for an alternative custody program that would allow him to finish his term on parole, wearing an ankle monitor. During a hearing to approve or disapprove his application, most of the review panel were in favor of allowing his parole, except for one important individual. "Everybody but the warden was on my side. The warden says, 'Why should I give you a chance? Why should I even think you're gonna succeed?'"

Eric told him about a possible opportunity to work at Kathy's House. "This is the first time in my life I want help and I want to change," he told the warden.

Eric left the room while the prison authorities talked among themselves. When he came back in, the warden said, "Look, this is what I'm going to do. I know you're gonna fail. I've been doing this for thirty years, but just to prove it to all these people, I'm gonna let you go, and I'm gonna laugh in all these people's faces when you fail."

"I got released to come to Kathy's House. And I'm here today with no problems. No, nothing—and not failing. I don't hate my heart anymore; I have peace."

Eric recently had his first interaction with his stepson, Chris, after a long separation. Chris hated Eric, with good cause. "I took Chris's girlfriend because she liked me more than him," Eric admitted. "I put my wife in a separate bedroom and moved Chris's girlfriend in with me. We were all in the same house. This is the kind of crap I dragged my wife and son through. I've done this two or three times. I have beaten this kid up. He had every right to hate me.

"I was an ugly, ugly person. I didn't care if you didn't like it. Did not care. I put no value on people, nothing. I could take somebody's life and go eat. It made no difference to me. I mean, it was nothing. Life had no meaning to me. I didn't care if I died, so why would I care if I killed you? That was my mentality."

Chris told his mother if he ever saw Eric again, he would kill him. Jonathan Phillips picked up Chris because he was in a desperate condition, homeless, strung out, all his teeth broken.

Jonathan knew that Eric was working at our house. "They had just picked up Chris, and Jonathan said he was going to bring him over to the house to work on a fence.

The kid got out of the car. He looked at Eric, and I thought, "Oh no. I'm glad nobody has a gun." And all of a sudden, they both started crying. They went and hugged each other for about ten minutes. There was total and complete reconciliation.

"Now I love that kid to death," Eric said. "I'm thankful for forgiveness. I pray for him every morning in tears. Thank you for the reconciliation. It's amazing."

Eric has been involved in helping our ministry since his release from prison. "I can count on J.P. and Diana for anything. I know they got me. Their ministry has bent over backward to help me. The Lord just surrounded me with all these great people. Now I have feelings toward my wife, and my marriage is amazing. His mercies are new every morning."

Chapter 27

The Call To Pakistan

In 2012, we were riveted by a guest speaker from Pakistan at Heritage Church in San Clemente. Pastor Tariq (name changed for security reasons) had been hiding in the U.S. from the Taliban, apparently because the terrorist group had placed a fatwa on his head.

A fatwa can be any ruling about Sharia law issued by a mufti, or Islamic judge. Fatwas came to world attention after Ayatollah Khomeini released a fatwa against author Salman Rushdie, condemning him to death because of his novel *The Satanic Verses*, which was considered blasphemous by Islamic religious authorities.

We gave Pastor Tariq the second service to preach. He started bawling like a baby as he described the spiritual condition of Pakistan, with more than 200 million people who have never heard the Good News about Jesus. As he spoke of the need for Christian education and the plight of Christians working in brick factories, our hearts were profoundly moved. Pastor Tariq talked about the need for a Christian influence to counter a culture where fundamentalist Islamic ideology is deeply rooted, and a significant portion of the population becomes radicalized.

A few weeks after his talk, the Taliban leader who ordered the fatwa was killed by a U.S. drone strike, and Tariq was able to return home to his wife and three children.

After Tariq left, we sought the Lord to get personally involved in Pakistan. He was the catalyst for our decision to move in this new direction. We believed this would become our mission: to make disciples of the world. We didn't realize at the time it would involve a risk to J.P.'s life to fulfill God's desire to save His people.

We knew God would never give us more than we could handle and would always provide the tools to do the job He called us to do. We rested in this Scripture: *"And my God shall supply all your need according to His riches in glory by Christ Jesus"* (Philippians 4:19).

First visit, 2014

Pastor Roger Gales and another man, Toby Ray, made the first trip to Pakistan, representing Heritage Church, to verify the needs described by Pastor Tariq. "We just went to explore," Pastor Roger recounted. "There was no agenda. Tariq showed us a bunch of different needs. Toby and I followed Tariq around for a week. It was moving to see all the suffering of the Christians there."

Pastor Tariq took them to see several brick factories where Christians were laboring in a form of indentured servitude that many would say amounts to slavery. As they drove out of the big city into rural areas, they could see large brick chimneys dotting the landscape, each one indicative of a place where bricks are fired.

Every brick in that country is made by a Christian slave because Muslims will not do that kind of work. The Christian population is largely illiterate because they are not allowed to attend schools. Many of the schools have large banners declaring "No Christians are allowed to attend this school." Since they are uneducated, it is difficult for them to enter the workforce. Christian parents, faced with their inability to feed their children, will often sell their children into servitude with the belief that it is the only way to prevent them from starving.

About eleven million Christians work in the brickyards alone, with textile mills employing most of the rest. Nearly every building in Pakistan is built with bricks and 100 percent of the bricks are made by Christian slaves. When a Christian slave marries, the children become the property of the slave owner.

Pastor Tariq told him there are approximately 56,000 brick factories in Pakistan alone—all functioning with Christian slaves.

I (J.P.) learned this system has been going on for generations. The slave owner has phony books—a book of debtors—where he charges them for food and shelter. When government officials ask the owners why they have no payroll, they show them their debtors book and explain that all the people working onsite owe them money and are working off their debt.

Not only do they stay enslaved by his books, the debt grows and passes along from generation to generation. They inherit the debt of their parents and grandparents.

While it is against the law there to have slaves, the harsh reality of their indentured servitude amounts to functional enslavement. It is also against the law for a child to work, but the brick factories are full of children making bricks. The government looks the other way at many of the abuses that go on.

I later discovered a typical family of four has a quota to make 2,000 bricks a day, working seven days a week from sun up to sun down. There are no days off. They can do it, but they have to work very hard. If they don't meet their quota, they don't eat. They receive one meal a day, usually rice. Some believe the slave owners treat their animals better than they treat their Christian slaves—and they don't hesitate to beat their animals.

> *"'Therefore go now and work; for no straw shall be given you, yet you shall deliver the quota of bricks.' And the officers of the children of Israel saw that they were in trouble after it was said, 'You shall not reduce any bricks from your daily quota.'"* (Exodus 5:18-19)

When Pastor Roger visited the first brick factory, he was surprised there was no gate or security guard in place, and he didn't see anybody in chains. "I didn't know what to expect. But one thing they have in common is that they're all Christians who work there.

"They live on the premises. The adults do the hard work of digging the mud and putting it in wheelbarrows. The stronger people do that work. And then the women or younger people make the bricks and dump them upside down. And then the little kids turn them over in the baking sun. And so, everybody in the family works. The kids were playing and splashing in the water at some of the places, but they had a quota to meet every day, which is a lot of pressure, and that's why the entire family works. And it is shocking to see how young the kids are who are turning bricks over. As soon as you're about three to five years old, old enough to stay focused on the task, they begin to work.

"The kids turn a brick over, step forward, turn a brick over, step forward, turn a brick over ... There were a few trees they could rest under, but for the most part, they work in the sun all day long." And it never stops, month after month, year after year."

As Pastor Roger toured the flat, parched, sunbaked land where the bricks were being made, he noticed a group of about five children under a tree and approached them with Pastor Tariq, who began to translate for them.

"I remember a girl in a red dress. There were two girls, and they were about ten years old, inseparable, holding hands together," Roger recounted.

"And the girl in the red dress said, 'Uncle, can you please rescue us? Please take us with you ... I don't like this place.'"

Pastor Roger felt compassion for her beleaguered condition but knew he couldn't do anything at that moment. Then Tariq said gently, "Not now, dear ... someday."

After Roger and Toby returned home, they shared about their trip with the elders, and they began to pray about how the church would help. The elders in faith decided that we would attempt to build a school. Tariq said a school would be the biggest need, the biggest challenge, and the most money, and yet the most effective thing we could do to bring a lasting impact.

As Pastor Roger prepared to communicate the need to the church the following Sunday, he learned the identity of the little girl in the red dress who asked about leaving. Her name was Miriam.

He presented the need at church, showed some slides from the trip, and related the way his heart was touched by Miriam. He challenged them to give generously to the new school building project, and the response overwhelmed him. "One woman gave me a check for $40,000 right there on the spot," he recalled.

Roger called Tariq the next day. "I have the money to break ground!" he said excitedly.

Pastor Tariq was overjoyed and elated. In the phone conversation, Roger said, "Take some of the money and rescue Miriam."

"Okay, I'll go this week and do it," Pastor Tariq replied.

A "rescue" entailed negotiating with the factory owners, which meant Tariq would purchase Miriam for the debt she owed to her family. Once "redeemed," Pastor Tariq would place her in a family within his circle of churches.

A few days later, Tariq called back with horrible news. He went to the brick factory to arrange for her release and discovered she died the night before of Dengue fever. The two pastors wept together on the phone. "We both cried and cried on the phone, and I said, 'Okay, well, then go rescue her girlfriend in the blue dress.'"

The following Sunday, the church service in San Clemente was very powerful. Pastor Roger spoke. "I shared with the congregation that Miriam had died and said it was very moving for me and sad, and the whole congregation was moved.

"It's too late for Miriam. We can't do anything for her, but there's an urgency for the children that are there," he said.

Then something unexpected happened. I had been sitting in the front row. I stood up and walked toward Roger and asked if I could have the microphone. Roger said, "This was not protocol, but I trust J.P., so I handed him the mic."

"Well, Diana and I were just sitting there talking," I began. "And we said, 'We're gonna give $5,000.'" Then I looked at Roger and said, "Roger, will you and your wife give $5,000?"

Put on the spot, Roger's mind began to race. *I don't have $5,000*, he thought, *but I have a motorcycle that's probably worth exactly $5,000.*

"Yes, we can give $5,000," he said.

Then I turned to the audience and said, "Who else here will give $5,000?" Hands began to shoot up all over the room as I said, "Thank you, thank you, thank you …"

I launched into fundraising mode. "Okay, who's going to give $1,000?" Now, many more people raised their hands.

"After the service, people came up to me with checks, lots of checks," Roger recounted. "Some people gave cash. The same thing happened in the second service. It wasn't as spontaneous as the first service, but it was the same idea. These weren't pledges over the next twelve months. After the second service, I held this wad about four inches thick with cash and checks, which, for the size of our church, was a significant amount of money and sacrifice. I know people were sacrificing. That day, we raised about $200,000 for the school."

We caught the vision and began to respond ourselves. We committed to change the direction of our lives, to help others become free from slavery and abuse. Diana sold the shelter for women, which had been her life's purpose for twenty years. She moved the office into our home, and we hunkered down for an unknown future. Along with the church, we began to raise funds to send to Pakistan to build two schools and to rescue our Christian brothers and sisters.

They responded to the Lord's call and challenged others to quiet their hearts and listen for God's next ministry assignment. "Is there a journey in you?" Diana asked. "Have you heard the sweet whisper of God in your ear? Do you have a gift to share with others? Our lives are precious, and we don't know how much time is left for us to venture out to do what the Whisperer is saying … The sweetest sleep comes from obeying God."

CRACKED VESSELS

Chapter 28

Second Pakistan Visit

In 2015, I (J.P.) made my first visit to Pakistan with another man from Heritage Church, Patrick Moy. After we arrived, we were very exhausted and jet-lagged. I preached Sunday morning and didn't have a decent night's sleep beforehand. There were virtually no chairs in the church, so everyone either stood or sat on the floor, including older people.

As I glanced around the church, I noticed bodyguards with AK-47s standing in strategic locations because of a rise in persecution throughout the country.

In 2012, a mob of protesters in Mardan, a city in northern Pakistan, set fire to a church, along with an adjacent church school, library, computer lab, and the homes of four pastors. The following year, Muslims attacked a Christian neighborhood in Lahore and burned more than 100 homes according to a report by *France 24*.[1] Only a short time before our trip, *Geo News* reported separate blasts targeted two different churches on the same day during Sunday services near Lahore. Eyewitnesses said a man blew himself up outside one of the churches as a police guard stopped him from entering, while the other blast took place inside the church during Sunday mass. At least fifteen people were killed and seventy wounded in the attacks.[2]

So, the placement of the bodyguards seemed prudent and entirely necessary to me under the circumstances. Later, at the Sunday evening service, a Muslim couple came carrying a baby paralyzed from birth. They told the story about seeing the TV program, and so they brought him up and asked me to pray for him. The mother's head was covered. When they came up, the baby was stiff as a board. His eyes would move but nothing else. He was about a year old. I prayed a very piss-poor prayer. I had no energy, and neither did Patrick. I said, "God, would You please touch this baby." I didn't even share the gospel with the family, and I knew they were Muslims. I was just out of it.

After I prayed, the couple sat down behind me, so I couldn't see them or the baby. Then God did something remarkable.

I started preaching, and it didn't take very long before no one was looking at me. Suddenly I turned around and looked, and that baby started moving! I stopped preaching as everyone began to gather around the couple. It was really exciting. They were holding him up, and his head was bobbing all around. It was an amazing miracle of God ... it happened!

On the trip, I learned Pastor Tariq himself had once been a slave in a brick factory. He was an orphan rescued by a Christian Pakistani couple who purchased his freedom. Brought up in a relatively affluent environment, he received a good education and had no financial worries. One of his best friends became a parliamentary leader representing Christian causes.

There are 600 seats in the Pakistani Congress, and only three seats are reserved for Christian representatives. His friend tried to change the laws that make slave ownership legal. He was martyred—killed by the Taliban. His body was burned and stuffed into a fifty-five-gallon drum. They brought his body to Pastor Tariq as a warning. Tariq has been following in his friend's footsteps ever since. He confesses he has moments of fear for himself and his family, but he has more moments of faith and confidence he is doing the will of God. He has a great heart!

After the dramatic healing of the baby, Pastor Tariq told us about a local Al-Qaeda cell that had placed a fatwa on his head, along with other Christian leaders. The cell group went to hear Tariq preach, and one of the guys concealed a gun under the big, baggy clothes they wear. After Tariq quit preaching, this guy went up and had the gun underneath his clothes. He attempted to fire it, but the gun jammed.

That night something amazing happened. The gunman went home, went to sleep, and in his dreams, Jesus revealed Himself as the Man in White. After the man awakened, he told the other men in his Al-Qaeda cell what happened. Within two weeks every one of them had the same dream!

They knew where Tariq lived, and they went to his compound where there was a school and his house. You couldn't drive through the street. In front of the compound is a big iron gate. On the second floor of the girl's school, there were guards all the time with machine guns. They were no more than a mile away from a Taliban mosque.

One of the guards ran to warn Tariq about the men approaching. "What should we do?" the guard asked. Tariq sent his wife and children up on the roof to hide, and he went with the guard to investigate.

When Tariq saw the men, they appeared to be unarmed and did not seem threatening, he invited them to come in. They entered and proceeded to tell about having similar dreams. "Who is the Man in White?" they wanted to know.

Tariq led them to the Lord, they got baptized in the Holy Spirit, and he washed their feet.

Later I told Tariq I would like to meet these men. One day Patrick and I were at Tariq's house in the morning, and he said the former Al-Qaeda men would be coming to breakfast.

"Do you want to meet them?" Pastor Tariq asked.

All of a sudden, I got cold feet, and so did Patrick. *If there is one mole, we could all be dead.*

The men arrived and began to have breakfast downstairs, while Patrick and I paced upstairs, still hesitant about the encounter. Finally, we decided to let faith swallow our fears. When we walked downstairs, we could hear them singing. We opened the doors, and these guys looked like terrorists, but they had big grins on their faces and began hugging us.

I have a picture of the guy holding the gun that jammed, and he is giving it to Tariq. We spent three hours with them. Every one of them is underground now in Pakistan. They haven't even contacted their spouses for fear they would get killed. They wanted to get together with them again. They were also afraid if they went around their families, their families would be hostile.

Chapter 29

Third Pakistan Visit

In 2016, I was turned down twice for a visa to return to Pakistan. I finally went to the consulate in Los Angeles and shared my heart about the school with a consular official. The official appreciated my compassionate desire to help the children and expedited my visa.

Pastor Roger and I flew to Pakistan to see the school built with the money we raised, a total of $296,000. One portion of the money came from an unexpected source. Josh McDowell, the noted apologist, evangelist, and author, donated his lifetime collection of ministry memorabilia from his extensive travels, which were auctioned during one weekend at the church.

The money we raised built the school and paid for two years of operating expenses. The K-12 Christian school accommodates 2,000 students.

The government changed, and the new government would not allow boys and girls to attend the same school. We proposed teaching boys upstairs and girls downstairs. We also proposed teaching on separate days. But the government said absolutely not. They said boys and girls had to be in completely separate facilities. So, we committed to raising money for building a girls' school. We already owned the land.

We learned that when we were building the school, somebody ran off with $5,000 or $10,000. Pastor Tariq called me and told me about it. He was very sorry and explained how it happened. My thought was to thank him for being honest. In any project in any country, there's a risk that somebody's going to cheat you. And losing $5,000 or $10,000 in that context was probably really inexpensive. In all these situations, Pastor Roger followed President Reagan's maxim: trust, but verify.

"I always questioned what was happening," Pastor Roger admitted. "I wondered about Tariq's credibility all the time. I have done ministry in some other countries. Whenever you're contributing American dollars, you're almost guaranteed corruption. It almost always goes south. So I was cautious always."

After we arrived, we were impressed with the lightning-fast progress made in constructing the school. Pastor Roger described visiting the school: "Once they have the money in hand, they can build very quickly. The school was done, it was finished, and it was beautiful. There were a lot of students there. We got to see the students and got to meet the teachers. We went through the classrooms. It was obvious it was a well-run school built with our donations.

"It was a victory lap more than an inspection," he recalled. "They treated us like rock stars. We didn't want to be treated like that, but they did it anyway. And we specifically asked them not to do that."

On the trip, we visited three brick factories. I remember one woman holding a baby while she worked. The baby looked like he was going to die. The baby's father, Simon, had three fingers and a thumb cut off his right hand. He only had one remaining finger on his hand to make bricks.

I told Pastor Tariq I wanted to get that family out. So they paid the family's debt and set them free. That family remains very special to me. I've seen them every trip. The church bought Simon a donkey and a donkey cart and paid for two months' rent on an apartment. He started picking up trash, then graduated to selling produce on the corner. Then he graduated to supplying restaurants and produce companies. Soon he was making more than enough to support his family.

After witnessing the joy of setting human beings free, God impressed something momentous on my heart: *This is what I want you to do for the rest of your life.*

We raised money for that specific purpose. It was our first experience of actually sitting down with slave owners and negotiating for the workers' freedom. In total, we delivered sixty people from slavery on our trip.

In one brick factory we got twenty-eight people out for free because we always have a video going and cameras. The owner didn't want us on the property. He said to take them and leave. He thought maybe we were from the BBC or some news agency. The average redemption price was $600 to $700 per family.

Chapter 30

The Miraculous Fourth Visit

The "miraculous" fourth trip in 2017 came together after Pastor Tariq informed the church in San Clemente that a certain Taliban leader named Usama, who owned twenty-eight brick factories, was being pressured by the government to close some of them down.

He committed many atrocities. One of his henchmen threw an eleven-year-old boy down a well and drowned him. The mom and dad were crying and wanted his body. They pulled the body up but wouldn't give it to the family. They doused the boy's body with gasoline and burned him right in front of his parents. They threw the boy's body in the brick kiln.

There will be no justice for these parents. He (the Taliban owner) considers him just another infidel who died.

Before this, the Pakistan Parliament passed a law preventing children under fourteen from working in the brick factories. Based on the new law and serious human rights violations, Usama was ordered to shut down sixteen kilns and convert his land to some other use. He sold his property to the Taliban, but he could not sell his slaves along with the property because human trafficking is illegal in Pakistan.

Pastor Tariq informed us the government had been watching Usama, and he was in a hurry to flee the country before he was indicted for his crimes. The walls were closing in on him. He needed to make a quick deal and get out of town.

The seller's urgency provided the opportunity to free thousands at a fraction of the going rate. In the email sent to the church, Pastor Tariq said there were 584 families they could free from slavery at the factories, approximately 4,500 people. He thought they could get them out for $250 per family.

A one-week trip was proposed, but I questioned whether we could accomplish everything in such a short time. After wrestling with the logistics, I decided to go. I was going to go by myself. I couldn't get anybody to go with me because it was short notice.

At the last minute an Orange County businessman, Mark Williams, who also attended Heritage Church, decided to travel with me. Mark said, "It took me a couple of days to come around, but the opportunity to help so many was too enticing for me to pass up. It was confirmed that we should go when we were able to get our visas in one day.

"All I can say is that throughout history God has chosen the most unlikely people to get things done," he added.

Diana was amazed at how quickly the trip came together. "We raised money on a Sunday at church, and J.P. and Mark got on a plane on Monday. We had no idea how much money there was—we hadn't even counted it yet. We were just sending them in faith."

The security situation in Pakistan was something both of us men weighed carefully, including travel warnings issued by the U.S. State Department. "The Pakistani Government was trying to reduce the violence, but terrorists still operated out in the open," Mark noted. "It is generally safe if you are Muslim, but for the rest of us it is best to travel with security."

The Taliban were not attempting to hide their operations. "The Taliban openly identify by dressing in green and white and identify their mosques by painting the domes green," Mark said. "Outside the shops of Taliban sympathizers are donation boxes with signs that say

'Buy a bullet, kill an American.' Taliban volunteers set up illegal tollbooths on the roads to collect money for jihad. Terrorist training camps operate right by the road in plain sight."

Because of the dangers that existed and the desire of the Pakistani Government to keep U.S. aid flowing, Pastor Tariq was provided with police protection. "He also has a security staff that travels with him everywhere he goes. Because of our mission and the fact that we were dealing directly with the Taliban, there were some situations where our human security force was probably not enough. Fortunately for us, our safety was in God's hands," Mark said.

In our journey, this Scripture brought us assurance:

> So do not fear, for I am with you; do not be dismayed, for I am your God. I will strengthen you and help you; I will uphold you with my righteous right hand. (Isaiah 41:10 NIV)

Pastor Tariq met us at the airport with five security guards. They had to check their AK-47s with airport security, but security gladly returned them as we were leaving the parking lot. On his previous visit, Pastor Tariq brought flowers with him to greet me, but this time he arrived empty handed.

"Where are my flowers?" I asked, feigning disappointment.

"I'm sorry I didn't bring them," Tariq stammered, "but I ran out of time." He went on to explain he had to go by the brick kiln to pick up the bodies of two ten-year-old girls that had been raped and beaten to death. One of them had been beheaded, and no one made any effort to bury the girls, so Tariq buried them himself.

The day they arrived was the start of Ramadan, the month-long period of fasting by Muslims that commemorates the revelation of the Quran to Muhammad. "The roads were mostly empty," Mark recalled. "Even so, we still experienced 100-mile-an-hour speeds and plenty of horn honking. Anywhere we stopped, the guards rolled out from our escort vehicle and formed a circle around us. The amazing thing is that no one seemed to think this behavior was odd. Nearly everyone who can afford it travels with security, and no one seemed to be the least bit intimidated by our massive amount of firepower."

On the way into town, we drove by the Christian cemetery where Pastor Tariq had just buried the two girls. "The cemetery was run down and dirty," Mark recounted. "Directly across the street was the Taliban Mosque. No expense was spared on that building. It was easily the nicest building we had seen in Pakistan."

As we spent more time with Tariq, we increasingly understood and were dismayed by the plight of Christians working in the brickyards. Failing to meet their quota for bricks would result in no food for the day and possibly a beating. Additional failures can result in severe beatings or torture so that the rest of the slaves will be intimidated and work harder. Typical discipline can include having fingers, hands, or forearms chopped off. Chronic low production has resulted in slaves being burned alive in the brick kiln, even though the lack of output may have been the result of job-related injuries, illness, or disability.

"If the slaves cost the owner money for medical attention, they have no way to pay the money back. Sometimes, the owner will select one of the slave's family members as an organ donor and sell one of their kidneys to satisfy the debt," Mark discovered to his horror.

Sadly, sexual abuse is also rampant. "Young girls are set aside for the slave owner's personal use in addition to their daily brick-making duties. These girls have a wire in their noses to let everyone know that they are the personal property of the slave owner. Many of the girls we saw who had these special rings were nine or ten years old."

Additionally, the weather is often forbidding. "The brick-making areas are in open fields where temperatures can be as high as 120 degrees in the summer and below freezing in the winter. At night the Christians sleep in the same field where they worked all day. Often, they are shackled. Most have no jackets or blankets. It is not uncommon for them to freeze to death in the winter. Weather is no excuse for lost productivity and their only tools are a hoe, a cart, and a metal mold for forming the bricks. Everything else is done with their bare hands."

If these Christians don't work, they don't eat.

Jet-lagged, we got about two hours of sleep on our first night. In the morning, we set out to inspect the living conditions of families that had been rescued a few weeks before our arrival.

In addition to finding temporary housing with other church members, Pastor Tariq also raised money to purchase donkey carts for many of the families. "These carts are a versatile way to make money because they can function as a freight hauler, a taxi, or a fruit stand," Mark explained. "Anytime you see a donkey cart, you can be sure that the owner is a Christian. One of the men who received a donkey cart is making more than the principal at the school. He has electricity, a refrigerator, and a TV in his home. Every family has a different experience after slavery. Some take right to working or find instant success starting their businesses.

"Others are so broken that the only way they survive is through the support of others. The family that lost their eleven-year-old son who was thrown in a well also lost their daughter two weeks later. The father had arthritis that was so bad his knees were three times their normal size, and the mother was so emotionally damaged that she could no longer speak. The local pastors look after families like these, and the other Christians share what they can to keep them going."

That afternoon we visited the school built with the church's help. Not only was this school home to 1,500 kids, the certification of this school allowed them to open regional schools throughout Pakistan—many in brick kilns. We prayed for the teachers while we were there. We were disheartened to learn the teachers had not been paid in two months. They told us that they would rather work for free if it meant keeping the school open.

Later, we helped form a team to come alongside the school to sponsor teachers and provide financial advice so they could maintain greater fiscal stability.

...

On the morning of our third day in Pakistan, we received word that a total of $106,000 had been wired from California to a bank account set up locally, which meant they had adequate funds to rescue 4,500 slaves.

We set out to visit the brick kilns one by one. As we toured the grounds, I declared with unbridled enthusiasm, "We are planning to get you out tomorrow ... You made your last brick!"

Some were confused and couldn't comprehend what I was saying. When others grasped what was about to happen, they buried their face in their hands and wept—completely overwhelmed—as they dared to entertain the hope of a new day coming.

However, there was some degree of faith behind my dramatic pronouncement because we had not cemented our final deal with the Taliban leader who owned the factories.

"We told them we would be back the next day to pick them up and take them to their new home," Mark recalled. "Their kids would be able to go to school, and they would be able to get a job that they would be paid for. Then we told them to find a shady spot and take the rest of the day off."

For some families, the mission's success would mean the end of generations of slavery, the final curtain coming down on a multi-act, horrifying tragedy that seemingly had no end.

We strategized with Pastor Tariq how to handle logistically the large number of slaves to be freed at the same time. We decided we would collect them in one location where we would feed them and then transport them to their new homes. That afternoon we dispatched people with some of the cash that we had carried with us to arrange for transportation and food at the collection site.

In the afternoon, we visited one of the regional church schools. Other schools in the system were being run by Presbyterians, Methodists, Baptists, and the Salvation Army. Three of the churches agreed to take financial responsibility to house fifty families upon their release.

As we toured the grounds of the schools, we were greeted like royalty, with the children singing, dancing, and thanking us for assistance.

Later in the afternoon we went to the main brick factory where Usama had his office. We talked outside because there were so many security people on both sides we couldn't fit in his office. "I don't want to talk here," Usama told us. "I want you to come to my farmhouse at 6:00 tonight."

At a little after 6:00, the Taliban owner called and said he couldn't make it then but would call when he was ready. At 9:00 we started to get nervous.

"I'm afraid to go over there," I admitted to Pastor Tariq. "This guy is evil."

Pastor Tariq said he wanted to get the deal done that

night. Finally, the Taliban leader called at 9:30 and told us to come to his farmhouse. It was pitch black as we approached the man's home. A guard came out to the gate with a 57-magnum pistol.

As we pulled up, an amber porch light revealed other Taliban heavily guarded the house with AK-47s. I was in the lead car along with Mark, Pastor Tariq, and a security guard carrying an AK-47. A second car followed with three pastors on Pastor Tariq's board and another security guard. A third car was filled with four security guards equipped with AK-47s.

Usama's farmhouse was enclosed with a high fence and had a large inner courtyard. The gate to the courtyard was manned by three armed guards, and four more were inside the courtyard.

"There was a small office that was about 100 feet from the main house where they told us we were going to meet. The office had only one door, and Usama's bodyguard positioned himself in front of that door as soon as we entered the room. Our guards formed a perimeter behind his guards to discourage any bad behavior," Mark reported.

There were two windows without glass and a desk. The night air was heavy. Mark and I sat down, and Pastor Tariq stood at the end of the desk. The three pastors were standing against the wall. Their guards and our guards were standing around. The guy guarding the door was very evil-looking. The secretary looked very evil. The Taliban leader and his secretary sat on the other side of the desk.

Immediately the Taliban leader declared he wanted $1,000 per family—a dramatic increase over the agreed terms of $250. The secretary asked if Pastor Tariq brought cash with them.

"No, it's in the bank," Pastor Tariq replied.

The secretary turned red and pounded the table. "We want cash, cash, cash," he roared.

"You ought to give them to us for free because of all the money they've made for you over the years," Mark blurted out.

One of the Taliban leader's guards started shouting, then got up and stuck the barrel of his AK-47 against one pastor's throat.

This is going to be a bloodbath. I waited for the room to erupt in gunfire. Somehow, some way, nobody said anything else, and it calmed down. I have no explanation. A lot of prayer went into the meeting, and we were praying under our breaths.

Pastor Tariq turned to me and said, "Do you have anything to say?"

"How old are you?" I improbably asked the Taliban leader.

"Seventy-three," he said.

"I'm seventy-three." We stared at each other for a moment. "I am an honorable man," I said. "I came from America, but I was sent by God. God sent me over here to get His children free. You made an agreement with Pastor Tariq for $96,000. I'm not trying to get them out for $76,000. I'm keeping the commitment that he made to you to get God's people out of slavery.

"I will have to stand before God someday and give an account of how I've lived my life," I continued, sensing God's presence in the moment. I pointed directly at the Taliban leader. "You will have to stand before God someday and give an account of how you lived your life. I'm asking you right now to honor the commitment. We will write a check for $96,000, and you can go in the morning and cash it."

The Taliban leader studied me carefully, then nodded his head in approval.

To our great shock, he stood up abruptly, looked at me, and said, "Will you pray for me?" He put his hands next to his kidneys and said, "My kidneys are failing."

I stood up and placed my hand on the man's back and prayed an audacious prayer: "God, will You convict this man of all the horrible things he has done to Your people? Would You convict him of his sins? Would You, through the power of the Holy Spirit, reveal Yourself to him and save this man from all the things he has done, save his soul, and heal his kidneys?"

We wrote out the check to free the slaves and began hugging one other.

•••

The following day, we brought all the newly freed slaves together in one place, with a multitude of tarps offering shade. Pastor Tariq drove up in a Honda with us in the back.

It was like we were rock stars. They were touching the car. Old women were crying, wanting to shake our hands, little kids hugging us at the knees, and everybody got food.

It was the happiest day of my life. The magnitude of it—it's hard to explain. To see that many slaves set free ... I couldn't even fathom it. I went to bed that night and said, "God, nothing could top this."

At noon the next day, Pastor Tariq spontaneously decided to organize an evangelistic outreach for 9:00 that night.

I didn't think he would get anybody there. At 8:00 p.m. there were 200 people. Then cable TV and a guy with a drone showed up. By 9:00 the crowd had grown to 600 or 700. Then the band fired up, and amazingly, the crowd grew tenfold—to 6,000!

My eyes widened when the worship stopped, and

eleven Muslim clerics walked in. Pastor Tariq had invited them to come. He allowed the Shiites to use his church for their prayers on Friday.

The worship was very demonstrative, with people raising their arms and some dancing. The Muslim clerics were not participating. They were watching this.

Then Mark got up to preach. He had never preached before. Mark started talking about how to hear God's voice. His wife went to India a year ago, and he used her notes. He didn't realize it would be twice as long with a translator. He went fifty minutes, and it was close to midnight when he finished.

I was set to speak next. Pastor Tariq turned to me and said, "Make it short."

I only spoke for a few minutes, presenting the gospel in a simple, straightforward way. I talked about Jesus living inside a person. "Jesus can come in and change your life," I declared. "You can talk and pray to Him, and He answers your prayers. You can have this incredible relationship."

I allowed people to raise their hands and receive Christ. To the glory of God, several hundred raised their hands! I turned my head slightly and watched a Shiite cleric raise his hand. What's going on? I wondered.

Then I prayed for the sick. A woman came onto the stage asking for prayer because she was blind. When she still could not see after two rounds of prayer, she was persistent and asked for a third round of prayer. After the third prayer for healing, the woman cried out, "I can see! I can see!" She was miraculously healed!

The Shiite Muslim cleric who raised his hand came up to close the evening in prayer. He started preaching up a storm (declaring Jesus as the Messiah). Then Pastor Tariq tugged on his robe and whispered to him, "You're on TV, and you shouldn't be saying this." The man had received Jesus and wanted to tell the whole world!

The next morning Pastor Tariq received a phone call. One of the Muslim clerics wanted to come over to meet the American visitors. After he hung up the phone, Pastor Tariq explained that this man was a known terrorist, responsible for a plane going down.

"On the internet, he is identified as a terrorist," Pastor Tariq said. "I don't want him to come over," he informed us.

"But if he wants to kill us, he wouldn't call first. He would just come over and do it," Mark reasoned. Pastor Tariq changed his mind, called the man back, and invited him to come.

When the man arrived and I saw him, I was stunned. I looked at him and thought, this isn't the same guy I saw last night. He was grinning and crying at the same time, tears coming down his cheek. It wasn't the same guy.

Then the Muslim cleric shared an amazing story with us. For the last couple of years, it became apparent he had serious heart problems and needed a transplant. He was on the list for one.

The cleric watched and listened attentively to everything that happened at the evangelistic meeting. Nothing that was said or done seemed to penetrate his hard heart.

But after he went home and went to sleep, something remarkable happened. He had a startling vision of Jesus—the Man in White—who came to his bed as the Great Physician. Jesus began to do surgery on the cleric's heart.

When he awakened the next morning, he felt better than he had in years. He raced over to see his cardiologist, who performed some tests and came back with his head shaking, completely mystified.

"Your heart is normal!" the doctor declared.

Overwhelmed by the vision and the healing at the hands of the Great Physician, the Muslim cleric prayed to receive Jesus with Pastor Tariq and us. He was crying, like a big old ball of jelly. He grabbed and hugged me.

After I returned to California, I called Pastor Tariq, who said he was going to meet the former Muslim cleric that night. "He wants 1,000 Bibles in Urdu," Pastor Tariq said. "His wife has received Christ as her Savior. She saw such a difference in him."

"It is clear to see how God was showing His favor and protection over our ambassadors as they ministered," said Diana. "God is moving in powerful ways amidst a country that desperately needs Him."

*The new school in Pakistan,
built with funds from our church.*

*Our guide and the man who tried to shoot him,
but his gun jammed.*

This baby was prayed for during the meeting, and God healed his paralyzed body.

J.P. and Mark paying the slave owner for the slaves' freedom (for approximately 5,000 slaves).

CRACKED VESSELS

Chapter 31

Transitions

In 2020, I (Diana) sensed the time was drawing near for us to relinquish our full-time ministry roles. I was getting nearer to wanting to retire. One day I came home and was standing at the front door, and I felt like I was going to pass out. I grabbed the stair railing, and everything went black. I was not passed out to the point I didn't know what was going on, but I went black. I lay down on the floor. I couldn't get my legs to move, couldn't get up, couldn't walk.

After a minute or two passed, I regained my eyesight and called for help. J.P. rushed to my side and helped me to stand and walk to the bedroom. We quickly decided to drive to the hospital.

After doctors performed numerous tests, a doctor came into the room the next morning and delivered a grim assessment: "We believe you have what's called CAA, which stands for cerebral amyloid angiopathy. This involves inflammation in your brain. You also have proteins that are similar to Alzheimer's, but they're not Alzheimer's. You have your faculties. You can talk, you can reason, you can do things, so you don't show symptoms of Alzheimer's. But these proteins begin to weaken the blood vessels in your brain. And as they get weaker and weaker, we think you had an episode where you had a weak blood vessel that was in trouble—and it either leaked or burst. And that's when you hit black. There may come a day when the protein will cause a blood vessel somewhere to pop open, which will cause a stroke, and you could die."

"Oh my," I gasped. "Is there a cure?"

He shook his head. "No, there's no cure. It's so rare that I don't think I've seen more than a few people with this in my entire career. It is probably inherited."

"Really ... I don't think there's anybody in my family that has this. My mom had Alzheimer's, and she died from complications of that."

"Well, she could have had it and they didn't know, because diagnosing it is very difficult. And it's so rare that doctors don't know how to treat it."

"Can you do something to make the brain improve in some way?" I asked.

"No, we can't do anything."

...

A few months before my health crisis, Jonathan Philips, who came to Christ after years in prison and a visit with a witch, had begun to work with me as an intern.

His journey out of prison life and homelessness to become a productive, responsible contributor to our ministry team is emblematic of the way God used J.P. and I as His agents of transformation.

After Jonathan's release from prison, he returned to San Clemente but was unemployable. He was schizophrenic, strung out on meth and heroin. He wanted to get his three kids back. Initially, Jonathan found help through a ministry called I-Hope, a place where street people can get food, use showers, and access computers.

He started volunteering at I-Hope. He was living on the streets, but then his mother took him in. He didn't have a job because he wasn't very capable. But he told me that in prison he took a computer class.

Considering Jonathan's prison class, J.P. contacted an attorney named Dan and asked if he would consider hiring Jonathan to do computer input. He eventually became Dan's office manager. Dan said he had the best people skills of anybody he hired.

It was a large law firm, with 107 employees, and they began to downsize after Jonathan had been there for ten years. I heard Jonathan was not happy with what was happening internally. I was looking for someone to eventually take my place. I felt I needed to retire in the next few years, so I asked him to interview with Kathy's House. He said yes. I told him how much money he would be making, which was far less than what he had been making at the law firm. I told him he would have access to the men's ranch in Lake Elsinore and the women's home in Orange County, and eventually his income would improve.

Jonathan told us he was interested. "I was at the law firm for a decade," Jonathan said. "I knew it was not what I was supposed to be doing with my life. It was very profitable. But it was just not worth it, especially after the health crisis with my kidney. I wanted the rest of my life to count. I was working eighteen-hour days and taking too much time away from my family."

Jonathan sought the Lord's direction during a time of prayer and fasting and felt the Lord impress on his heart that He was preparing him to work in full-time ministry. In obedience, he stopped sending out technical resumes related to his computer background and began to send resumes to a few ministries he admired, including Prison Fellowship started by Chuck Colson.

By faith, he left the steady income of the law firm to find a position in ministry, but Jonathan began to feel the financial pinch of being unemployed. Was it foolish to jump away from a good salary before he had a new position in hand? He said, "We had significant bills because I had been making more and spending more.

One day, in response to a meltdown, Jonathan spoke out to himself. "We're so loved by God. He loves us so much. We're His kids, and He's not gonna let anything bad happen to us ... God, You're going to take care of us. You're going to come through for us."

After boldly and firmly declaring the truth of the Lord over his life, Jonathan stood up. His heart sank as he glanced at a pile of bills he had placed on his nightstand.

He walked over and picked up an envelope from Wells Fargo that he thought was a bank statement. He thought it might say he was overdrawn. "Dear Mr. Phillips, we're writing about your 2003 automotive loan with Wells Fargo Financial."

Jonathan wracked his brain but couldn't remember a loan with Wells Fargo. "I thought this was weird, and I started looking down the page. It said, 'We're sorry to inform you that we overcharged you through the life of this vehicle loan. To make it right, we would like to give you this check for $7,000.'

"The next day I got a call from Diana, and she said, 'Jonathan I'm feeling like it's time to retire, and I've been praying about you to replace me.'"

We got together and talked about the scope of the ministry and what Jonathan would be doing. "I just left a job making $120,000 a year, and I want to get a job in that range," he told her.

"Oh no, we're not anywhere close to that. We'll be lucky if we can start you at $35,000 or $40,000," I said.

This is impossible, Jonathan thought, even though he loved us and everything I told him. He said, "By that point, I had sent all these resumes, and Prison Fellowship got a hold of me and said they had a job opportunity in Deer Lodge, Montana."

There were over 600 applicants for the Montana position described as prison program development. "I kept praying Lord, Lord, if it's not meant to be, shut the door, and the door kept opening. I kept making it to the next interview and the next interview. Montana sounded appealing to me. So anyway, they offered me the job, along with $5,000 to help with the move."

When Jonathan broke the news to us, we cried together. "I love you guys so much," Jonathan told us. "This is a dream of mine to be in prison ministry, and I would like to pursue it. But I don't want to do it without your blessing."

"We're so happy for you," I said. "You know, you can get your kids out of here, you can own a home up there, and a part of us will go with you."

Jonathan got on a plane four days later and flew to Montana. The day after he left, I was rushed into the emergency room after I passed out by the front door. Jonathan remembered that moment: "I was in Montana while Diana was in the hospital getting an MRI, and they determined that her brain had bled. I had been talking to all these real estate agents looking for something to rent for our transition, and there was nothing, zero, available. My sixteen-year-old son called and said he wasn't going to Montana and would stay with his Mom.

Jonathan recognized God wasn't just shutting the door—He was slamming it. *Lord, why didn't You shut the door earlier?* he thought as he flew home to Orange County. *Why did I have to go all the way here?*

After he returned, he immediately went to meet with us. "I want to work with you," he said, his voice filled with emotion, "as long as you train me. I'm here, and I can't leave you. I'm committed to following this through."

Jonathan took a position with us for half what the other organization offered and a fraction of his previous salary with the law firm. "God made it work," he attested. "I don't even know how, but it's been miraculous, going from the lifestyle we were living to our current one. My quality of life has improved. When you say yes to God, He somehow makes everything work better. We're healthy, we have food, we're not doing an exorbitant amount of spending on junk like we used to. We don't go out to the movies all the time and all that stuff. We do things every once in a while and make them special."

Initially, Jonathan went to work for me as an intern to prepare to become the Executive Director of Kathy's House. I knew I was going to retire soon, but after I became ill, I just handed it over to Jonathan.

...

After the first episode when I collapsed at the door, we rushed to the hospital a second time in March of 2020 because I felt numbness in my face. I didn't want to have a stroke, and so I told my husband I needed to get checked out.

On the way to the hospital, we started singing the worship song "The Goodness of God" by Bethel Music.

After we got there, they examined me, and it took all day long for all the tests. I got near the MRI machine, and I was not in a good mood because they had a needle in me with contrast in it, and it was very painful. Before I went into the machine, the attendant asked, "What kind of music do you like?"

"I'm a Christian," I replied. "If you have the song, 'The Goodness of God,' I'd like to hear that."

"Sure, we have that one," the attendant said, surprising me.

I went into the MRI machine singing the song—anything to get my mind off the hideous metal clanging made by the machine.

As I was singing silently and thanking God for His goodness, something extraordinary happened. All of a sudden, the atmosphere changed, and I felt the most incredible wave of love I've ever felt in my life. It felt so complete, so nonjudgmental, like God loved everything about me.

"God, is this You?" I said without speaking out loud. Then a whisper said, *Don't worry. I'm going to take care of you.*

What does that mean? I wondered. "Lord, this is so wonderful what I'm experiencing," I told Him. "If this is what heaven is like, please take me with You. I don't want to stay here. Nothing in my whole life compares to the beautiful feeling I have right now."

Thankfully for J.P., God didn't grant my wish to be transported immediately to heaven. When the procedure finished, I was wheeled back into my room. Soon a doctor came in shaking his head in wonder. "You know what? The proteins are still there, but you have no more inflammation. It's all gone," he said.

"Wait, tell me again. I want to get this right. I have no more inflammation in my brain?"

"That's right—and your doctor is going to be so happy!"

In a follow-up with my other physician, he confirmed the lack of any inflammation. "What do you think caused that?" he asked.

"God met me in the MRI machine, and the feeling of love was so intense," I testified.

"Well, Diana," he said, "sometimes your result depends on having the right attitude." He was unwilling to attribute my miraculous improvement to a touch from God.

"I know it was God," I told him confidently.

A week later, I went in for another MRI test, this time for my heart. The attendant looked very young, and I asked him, "Do you know how to work this machine?"

"Oh, yeah, I went to school for a year to learn."

"Let me tell you what happened to me a week ago. I had another MRI, and it was for my brain," I began and then proceeded to describe my wondrous encounter with God.

"I'm so glad you told me that story because my grandma died a few weeks ago. I said to her before she passed, 'Grandma, will you come back and tell me if heaven is real? And is God real? Because I need to know that.' And then she died. And you just told me heaven is real and there is a God. I'm so happy to know the truth."

I brought the answer the young man sought from his grandmother!

J.P. marveled at the transformation in me since my encounter with God in the MRI. "From that day, she has changed and become a lot bolder. She will tell anybody who will listen what God has done in her life."

...

A few weeks later, I was recuperating at home, and I began sensing God speaking to my heart. "I was coming over every day," Jonathan said, "because she just got out of hospital. We're friends, we like to hang out."

When Jonathan walked through the front door, I exclaimed: "Jonathan, Jonathan, I heard from the Lord last night, and it was Micah 7:11: *'It will be a day for building your walls. On that day your boundary will be extended'*" (NASB).

Then the Lord impressed this question on my heart: *Why haven't you built My temple?*

I pondered the meaning of this for a moment, and then it hit me. God was speaking of the tabernacle within the human heart where the Holy Spirit dwells.

I believe He wanted us to have a home for men and build up the temple of God living within them. You know, take people off the street, wherever we can find them, and start building God's temple.

Three hours later, I was sitting in a car making an offer on a mobile home in San Juan Capistrano that would become a transitional home for men. They couldn't find a loan for the mobile home, but the seller lowered his price by $15,000. We paid cash for that mobile home, so the only output we have for that property is $242 HOA fees every month. That's it.

God had also placed a burden on my heart for homeless pregnant women. I didn't want them to get an abortion. God wants to save those babies, and He put that on my heart. I began to pray in earnest about the need.

A short time later, a pastor in Laguna Niguel who heard about our ministry called and requested a visit. Jonathan was here when Pastor Mike came over. Jonathan had attended their church, was impacted by their ministry, and even went on a mission trip to India with Pastor Mike. When Pastor Mike looked at Jonathan, it was like the prodigal son was home.

He couldn't get over the connection, divinely arranged by God. After we all sat down together, he said, "I've heard about what you're doing, and we're here to invest in your ministry. What would you like to do, Diana?"

"I want a home for women who are homeless and pregnant, but we can't afford the mortgage," I told him.

I talked about how we told a few people about our burden for the women, and some questioned whether the women in the streets were pregnant.

"Yes, they are," I explained. "They are just aborting before you realize they're pregnant. Seldom do you see a woman on the streets in her third trimester, because they abort the babies. We want to save the babies. We want to redirect their lives and tell them about God and save those babies."

Pastor Mike was taking it all in, and suddenly an inspiration from above lit up his countenance. "How about if our church buys a house. We will own it, but you can use it for your ministry for as long as you want. When you're done, we will take it back," he proposed.

I seized on the idea and said I already had found a condo for sale in San Juan Capistrano for about $516,000. "I can't believe that exists in San Juan Capistrano!" Pastor Mike exclaimed.

"It exists on my computer," I told him excitedly. A few hours later they placed an offer on the same condo. With some adroit maneuvering on the part of a Christian real estate broker in our church named Lon, they prevailed in a bidding contest against eleven other offers—and four of the competing offers were also cash.

There's no mortgage, so our only expense for the ministry is what it takes to feed them and utilities. God is so good. We have the income coming in from the thrift store to take care of that. Amazingly, God's provision here is that we have two places paid for. That is amazing! We found an overflow of blessings that resulted from obedience to God.

> *"'Bring all the tithes into the storehouse, that there may be food in My house, and try Me now in this,' says the LORD of hosts, 'If I will not open for you the windows of heaven and pour out for you such blessing that there will not be room enough to receive it.'"* (Malachi 3:10)

When Pastor Mike visited the home for women the first time, he said, "God is in this place! I sense the Holy Spirit is here."

I decorated it beautifully. The first pregnant girl who walked in said, "Oh my gosh, I have always dreamed of a house like this in the exact colors you did here." Every girl that comes in says they feel so special to be in that house.

We have an employee named Jeff Tyson who works the streets before he comes into our office in the morning. He talks to the homeless and tracks down rumors about pregnant street girls. If he finds a girl who is pregnant, we approach her and offer her housing and a chance to get out of the lifestyle on the streets. The problem with a lot of women is they can't get out of that life. They are unemployable and have been on the street so long. They're using drugs but want to get off them. We will take a single woman who is not on drugs if she is on the streets. We will take her to the rehab ranch if she is pregnant and on drugs. We have thirty women at the ranch right now. Pastor Mike also visited the ranch and was so impressed, he committed $1.5 million toward improvements to its infrastructure.

Later, we marveled at the way God put everything together. A big part of giving the money for the house and the ranch was Jon's obedience to God to bring Mike to talk to us. Isn't it amazing how God works? We are always in awe of that.

CRACKED VESSELS

Chapter 32

Beyond the Finish Line

In 2018, I (J.P.) made my last trip to Pakistan, accompanied by Jason Welch, the young man who lived in the streets as a drug addict, spent years in prison, and whose life was turned around by Jesus Christ with my guiding hand along the way.

After I extended the invitation to Jason, the younger man shook his head, unsure where he would find the money for the flight. That day I had an unplanned meeting with a woman named Lisa. We bumped into each other coming out of a store. She asked me about ministry needs, and I mentioned Jason's desire to go to Pakistan. She opened her purse, pulled out her checkbook, and wrote a check for the full amount of Jason's airfare.

Jason got so excited about Pakistan following their visit that he took the lead in launching another K-12 Christian school, which currently has eight teachers and is accredited by the government. His heart was also moved by the pastors he met on the trip, so he started an online Bible college to train pastors, with materials translated into twelve languages. Jason has also accepted speaking invitations in Haiti and the Philippines, where he has preached to thousands and seen many healings and salvations.

In 2019, I tried to obtain a visa for another trip to Pakistan, but my request was denied by the government. The COVID-19 pandemic shut down my trips over the next couple of years.

Due to death threats leveled against Pastor Tariq and his family, they fled to another country, where they now reside.

In reviewing our lives in ministry, we always stress that we are very ordinary people with many of the same struggles felt by other married couples. We've had a tumultuous journey because we are so different. But we appreciate so much about each other, and we love each other.

I (Diana) want people to realize we're nothing special. Everything we've done can be done by anybody who knows God and asks for help from God's Holy Spirit.

We've been through all kinds of trials. We have our moments when we're in the flesh and not following God. I don't want anyone who reads this book to think our life is perfect. I'm so thankful God uses the imperfect. We're "cracked vessels," and we would gladly admit that to anyone. God was faithful in every struggle to bring us back to doing things His way instead of ours.

And that's the beauty of knowing God—His forgiveness, His grace, and His love.

Final Thoughts

The process of compiling and writing these stories of God's hand in the lives of myself, J.P., and the people we've met has been a long and worthwhile one. To see the tapestry of hope and redemption God has woven into our lives laid out so plainly in this manuscript brought me to tears.

If there is one thing I want to leave you with, it is that *none* of this, not a single moment or miracle, was done through our strength, wisdom, or boldness. J.P. and I aren't special. We could never have known how to approach or even find these people on our own. But in the darkest moments, God whispers, and He holds our broken vessels, fortifies us, and reforms us to be submerged in His loving will and presence.

We are getting older and wanted to write this book as a memorial to what God has done so these stories can serve as a legacy of God's love and calling to share that love. We want our children, grandchildren, and great-grandchildren to be reminded of the legacy left to them, not by us, but by the One who made the lives we have lived possible.

This is your legacy, too, an invitation to not be complacent while waiting for God to wipe all suffering from the world, but instead to remember that you are here now. That you can be His hands and feel His touch in the process. There are no special requirements. J.P. and I just want to help people and obey God.

Our thanks to Arielle Anderson for helping me develop these final thoughts and our thanks to Mark Ellis, the founder of God Report's, for his assistance in putting together this book.

This excerpt is taken from an article written by Mark Ellis (May 2017) and shared on his website www.godreports.com. We encourage you to visit his website to finish reading the article.

Church with big vision frees 4500 slaves in South Asia, sees two Muslim leaders come to Jesus.

A church of 400 people in California undertook a big project – to build a school in South Asia. But one thing led to another and on their fourth mission trip to the unnamed country, two church members negotiated with a Taliban leader to free 4500 Christian slaves working at a brick factory.

They also participated in an evangelistic outreach that saw two Muslim clerics receive Christ. One of the imams had a powerful vision of Jesus as the Great Physician in the middle of the night following the outreach, which resulted in his miraculous healing and salvation.

It may have been the most productive short-term mission trip since Paul's visit to Macedonia.

Coincidentally, the man taking the lead on this trip was an unassuming 73-year-old retired businessman named Paul, aka "J.P." He had trouble finding another person in the church to go on the trip with him, but at the last minute, another self-effacing congregant, Mark, agreed to accompany him.

Underage boy stacking bricks

Afterword

My husband, J.P. (81), and I (78) are now what you would call "white hairs." We have both retired from our nonprofits and are trying to relax and enjoy our retirement time, but it is difficult to do since watching the chaos happening in the world and going to doctor appointments seem to take up so much of our time. So, we pray and ask God to show us opportunities to serve Him while we wait for His return.

Sometimes it's as little as picking up the daily newspaper and placing it on the front porch of a neighbor's home who struggles with immobility or pulling the trash can to the curb. It seems minor, but God knows what will help someone who struggles with pain.

We now have more grandkids than ever. Four children, ten grandchildren, and six great-grandchildren—whew! What a joy. Staying in touch with all of them is difficult. Visiting them is grand when we can see them.

We recently received a phone call from an old friend who helped us rescue 5,000 adults and children from brick factories in Pakistan. We were able to build two schools there, one for boys and one for girls. He shared that the schools are still active. Our five-year commitment to them was to pay the $8,000 per month needed for the teachers' salaries and other needs. After that, they had to start paying expenses. He said, "We have been able to meet the budget for three years now." That information brought us so much joy. God is meeting their needs!

Often, we get to see a life transformed by the love of God at the ministry homes for addicts and our rescue homes for moms and their unborn babies. Watching God at work in the lives of our residents builds our confidence that God is real. He hears our prayers and He loves us!

We hope as you read our real stories it will do the same for you.

J.P. and Diana

Endnotes

Chapter 2

1. John F. W. Dulles, *Yesterday In Mexico: A Chronicle Of The Revolution, 1919–1936* (Austin: University of Texas Press, 1989).

2. Jaymie Heilman, "The Demon Inside: Madre Conchita, Gender, and the Assassination of Obregón," *Mexican Studies/Estudios Mexicanos* 18, no. 1 (2002): 23–60.

Chapter 23

1. Peter Martell, *First Raise a Flag: How South Sudan Won the Longest War but Lost the Peace* (Oxford University Press, 2018).

2. Ibid.

3. Robbie Gramer, "'Our Worst Fears Have Been Realized': The Famine We Could Have Stopped in South Sudan," *Foreign Policy*, February 21, 2017, https://foreignpolicy.com/2017/02/21/our-worst-fears-have-been-realized-the-famine-we-could-have-stopped-in-south-sudan-united-nations/.

4. "Civil War Blamed for Starvation and Famine Looming in South Sudan," *Greene County Democrat*, March 29, 2017, https://greenecodemocrat.com/2017/03/29/civil-war-blamed-for-starvation-and-famine-looming-in-south-sudan/.

Chapter 28

1. "Protesters Burn Christian Homes in Pakistan," *France 24*, September 3, 2013, https://archive.ph/20130410201043/http:/mobile.france24.com/en/20130309-protesters-burn-christian-homes-pakistan.

2. "Two Blasts at Lahore Churches Claim 15 Lives," *Geo News*, March 15, 2015, https://www.geo.tv/latest/98175-two-blasts-at-lahore-churches-claim-15-lives.

CRACKED VESSELS

About the Authors

Diana

Diana graduated from the Police Academy at Golden West College in 1975 before serving as a reserve police officer at Fountain Valley Police Department. She later published several articles on various Christian topics for three Christian magazines as well as created and published "Denny's Ink," and in-house monthly corporate newsletter, for Denny's Corporation.

She cherished traveling to Washington, DC, to attend the inauguration of President Ronald Reagan, thanks to an invitation from her sister, Norma, who at the time was the Mayor of the City of Brea.

In 1997 she Founded Kathy's House, Inc., a faith-based shelter for women and children

in San Juan Capistrano, California. Later, in 2020, she worked to start a home for men addicted to drugs and alcohol in San Juan Capistrano as well as a home for pregnant women. All services provided in these homes have always been free.

Today Diana serves as President of the Board of Directors for Kathy's House and continues to help brainstorm ideas for the organization's growth with the new Executive Director, Jon Phillips.

J.P.

J.P. received a scholarship from Sweetwater High School for basketball at La Verne College in 1960. Due to changes in his life, he could not follow through with those plans and went instead to barber school.

His entrepreneurial skills kicked in as he began to purchase more barber shops. At last count, he had acquired twenty-eight shops by his twenty-ninth birthday, eventually selling each when the market was right.

Throughout his life, J.P. has served in a variety of pastoral and ministry roles:

- Associate Pastor for Believer's Chapel, San Clemente, California.
- Associate Pastor Ocean Hills Church, San Clemente, California.
- Associate Pastor for The Vineyard Church near Seattle, Washington.
- Founder and Pastor for United Community Outreach, a nonprofit providing food, clothing, housing, and teaching of God's principles in San Juan Capistrano, California.
- Founder of Lakeland Ranch (a branch of United Community Outreach), a discipleship program for addicts and alcoholics, housing up to fifty men and thirty women.
- Owner of La Tienda Thrift Store, Capistrano Beach, California, which provided the necessary funds to run all the shelters in Lake Elsinore, California, and help support Kathy's House.
- Mission Coordinator/Participant for the Pakistan ministry.

Besides God, J.P.'s second love is watching football, basketball, and boxing whenever and wherever he can.

www.ingramcontent.com/pod-product-compliance
Lightning Source LLC
Chambersburg PA
CBHW060522100426
42743CB00009B/1411